My Encounter

with the

Prophet of

GOD

ALBERT V. SALINAS JR.

ISBN 979-8-88943-681-2 (paperback)
ISBN 979-8-88943-682-9 (digital)

Christian Faith Publishing
832 Park Avenue
Meadville, PA 16335
www.christianfaithpublishing.com

CHAPTER 1

This is the story that changed my life. It all started in November 2018 on my mission trip to Trinidad and Tobago. I was to speak at the church of Pastor Vernie since this was my home church while I was there. I was getting ready for service as normal. I prayed and walked around this church in anticipation of a wonderful service. I later greeted parishioners as they came in the building. The time was getting close to start service, so I headed to my chair in the front row of the church. I started going over my notes so I would be prepared. A gentleman came and introduced himself to me as Pastor Robbie. As he introduced himself, he started to tell me four or five things about myself that nobody could've known. I was in sure amazement and puzzled at the same time. There was no way for him to know this about me since we had never met before in this life. Some prayers I haven't even told my wife about, he told me about at this encounter. I was now puzzled at how he knew all of this about. I had been praying for wisdom, knowledge, and understanding of God's Word. I also prayed to have someone to talk to in deeper revelation about God.

So my mind started going all kinds of different directions, trying to figure out how he knew all this about me. There is no way on earth he could know this about me. So I started trying to figure it out how he knew all this about me. He threw my whole sermon off, yet he said my sermon was pretty good. I don't believe that because I felt it was not my best effort due to the fact my mind was focused on him and how he knew things about me.

During my course of time there, I got to spend about twenty hours with him the remainder of my trip. During this time, we'd talked about many subjects and deep revelation of God's word. Sometimes I thought he was crazy. And other times I knew he was crazy. But we continued to talk and be able to bond. I wondered how he figured things out about me, and he told me it was easy. He said, before we came to earth, we signed a will. The will is what is between God and me. We both agreed what was to happen here on earth while we lived. It seems strange to me because I don't remember signing anything before I came here on earth. He told me it was because our memory was erased while we were in our mother's womb. Also, as an infant, we are learning all that we need to know while here on earth.

One day I was asking so many questions. He was frustrated and said, "Lord open his eyes so he can see. Remove a layer of scales off of his eyes so he can see the word." The next morning, I proceeded to read the word. And as I did, phrases and sentences started to pop out at me, like magic or revelation knowledge. I was so excited and amazed at the same time. I was eager to tell him the next time I saw him. And the next time I saw him was two days later. Before I could say a word, he said, "You sure were excited the next morning because your spirit woke up my spirit with excitement! So I knew you were able to see different things than the day before." And I was amazed and astonished by this new revelation and gift from God!

We had talked in the next year and a half about many topics in many deep subjects from the throne room of God.

At one point in time, I almost gave up on God because of the things he showed me. But I've pressed on, and the things that I know now have impacted my life more than anything else I've learned before my trip. I have learned about the power inside of me! And I now use the power inside of me to create things in my life. I am amazed still to this day and at how powerful we really are if we only understood the potential inside of us!

I'll give you an example of how it works. The formula to tap into this power is K plus V equals M. K stands for knowledge. V stands for vision. M stands for manifestation.

So how all this works is, he must have the knowledge and vision so our manifestation can happen. I tested this out on my daughter Megan. At the time she lived in Mississippi and said she would never move to Texas because she hated it here, I told her, if she moved, I could help her since she would be close to where her father lived. So I visioned her moving to Texas, but I held that vision in check until I made sure where she was to move to. I didn't think anything about it for about a week or two. Then out of the blue, she called and told me, "Dad, I'm moving to Texas!" I was in shock. But at the same time, I knew it was going to happen because that's what I visioned, and it came to pass.

Another example was my daughter from Tyler called and told us that her husband's boss was in a coma and was brain dead, living on life support. She asked us to pray for the family because they would be making the toughest decision in their life. If they pulled the plug, he could die. If he did not die, he would be a vegetable the rest of his life. Those were the two possible outcomes. Kathy and I prayed for him on that Friday that he would not be a vegetable or die but that he would live and be made whole! We called our daughter two days later and asked what happened to him.

She said she was scared to call but that she would call and let us know. She called back in amazement! She said they pulled the plug, and he came to recognizing everybody in the room! He wasn't dead or a vegetable but totally healed! The power inside of us to believe the theory and applied it toward his life! It really works. He wouldn't be alive today if it didn't. So if we don't put it into practice what God said we could do, why do we believe in God? What good is to hear the word and never apply the word of God?

I have come to the conclusion that God lives in me and I in Him. We are one with God. He lives in me, and I live in Him, so we are one. The same power that Jesus has, I also have. That is why, when I prayed with Kathy, the guy was healed. My daughter moved from Mississippi because I believed it, seen it happen, and it happened. We do have power inside of us, yet nobody has explained this power to us. What I will be trying to do is show you how to tap into this power. I will be using scripture and examples of how this has affected not only my life but other lives around me. So let us start this journey on understanding God and how He affects our lives!

Our mind is so powerful that we can trick ourselves into healing our own body! We have the placebo effect on ourselves. We can take a pill that is nothing but a sugar pill and believe we're taking human medicine. Our mind is tricked into thinking we are healed because of the medicine, but in reality, it's a trick that our mind believes. This is nothing new, as medical research backs this evidence on a continual basis. We are just slow to understand how this works. Our mind is capable in doing incredible things if we learn to let it. It's a powerful tool that is being fought for by God and the enemy. They need your energy to survive and thrive in the universe.

Once we understand this, we can start to understand how God works in our lives. We are being taught that God is the ruler of our universe and understands us, but we have no power, that all power comes from Him, and we are helpless. But in reality, we do have power. Our power can change our destiny and our world. So don't be surprised as you try these things. I will show you that they become a reality in your life. I'm not gonna motivate you to do or to believe certain things without evidence from my life or from somebody's life I know. You will be able to see and demonstrate how God works in your life!

So God created the world by speaking it into existence. So if we are the children of God, then we have the same qualities and traits as our Father. We are able to create things with our words. We have the capacity to create the things we want with our words. We must have the knowledge to know how powerful our words really are and how they create things in our lives. Don't get carried away speaking negative things in your life and wondering why you have negative things happening to you. You have spoken these things into existence. So we must choose to speak positive things into our lives so that positive things will happen to us! "We reap what we sow" also has to do with what you say. The verse doesn't only represent money sown and then reaping what you sow with money, but it pertains to your words as well. We have to realize how important it is what we say. In Proverbs, it speaks about how the tongue is a rudder, telling him which direction the ship must travel. So we must be careful with our tongue, or we could end up in a place we didn't want to in our lives.

Today is March 2020.

Today I'm going to write about my encounter with a prophet. I encountered this prophet for the first time in Trinidad. I was amazed at what was spoken to me and spoken about. He named things that I had been praying about for quite some time. I have never met this person before, yet he revealed things to me that he shouldn't have ever known about me. At first I freaked out when this happened. But as time went by I became more comfortable knowing that God cares about me. This was truly an encounter with God and His prophet. We read all the time in the Old Testament about prophets who helped do God's work, but to actually meet one is a whole different thing. And when I met him, it was amazing. We've talked for hours upon hours since then, and I am still amazed and still learning the things of the kingdom of heaven. God is just so unlimited in His teaching that we can't comprehend everything about Him!

I have been so blessed coming across God's prophet that I can't stop thanking him for all he does for me. The teachings that I am learning, the wisdom which is being revealed to me, and the power that lies within me just blow my mind! To think of how good and merciful God is and how He shows us His love and compassion in everything in this world.

How do you react to something that you have never experienced? As a pastor, I have read and studied the Bible. But then, you come across something that is something of a myth. I know that God says, "He is the same yesterday, today, and tomorrow," yet I have actually encountered this prophet who came into my life. The way I encounter was quite unusual to me, yet I don't know why I am so amazed at what happened since I prayed it, and God answered my prayers. One of the things I had been praying for was a deeper level of understanding of God's Word, a person who could guide me and lead me in truth of God's Word, also to give me wisdom, knowledge, and understanding of God's Word. I thought it was a simple enough prayer at the time, months before I went to Trinidad to preach. Well, let me tell you something. I got exactly what I prayed for, and I believe more, so much more! You would think, as a pastor, that I would have believed God answers prayers. I did believe God answered prayers, but this was so different. I have had prayers that weren't answered before, so maybe I was expecting nothing to happen like so many times before thinking that God wasn't gonna answer my prayers again. I understand that sometimes He doesn't because we aren't ready for the answer or God has something better for us if we will be patient and wait for the timing to be just right. Well, that's where I was, not expecting something supernatural to happen on this trip for me. I was the pastor coming to a foreign country to bless the people there. I knew something wonderful was going to happen because God had prepared a message for the Sunday before I left with music for my mission trip months in advance. I had let the pastor there know I needed this particular song, Elevation Worship's "Here as in Heaven." This song was chosen months ahead of time to be played, and God was going to do something different, but I didn't know what it was. Sunday service was amazing, and what happened was that God used me to change the atmosphere there in that church. And something inside of me was changed. I had changed that week, and I haven't been the same since! I got to encounter the prophet of God on that trip and haven't been the same since.

When I first encountered the prophet of God, it was right before I was going to minister on a Thursday night, like five minutes before service was going to start. He introduced himself to me and blew my mind by telling me what I had been praying and a couple of others things that had my mind spinning. I had to try to focus after this, and my mind was preaching when it was time to preach, but I was also thinking how he did know all these things about me when I had never met this man before in my whole life. I know I didn't do my best that night because my mind was in two places at the same time. I believe, after service, my head was still spinning, wondering about this man. The next day, the pastor had a gathering at the hosting pastor's house, and he was invited along with a few others to eat and fellowship. I spoke with this prophet for about six to eight hours that night, along with others who were privileged to listen to him. Some of the things he said were, let's say, unbelievable at the time. I wondered if he was a man of God or just a crazy man who had a good education and a very good imagination. I recorded some of the conversations to listen to later on because the topics were quite interesting and intriguing. We talked about God. The angels in heaven and some angels came down and visited us that same night, and the prophet was impressed. He told me how he knew so much about my past, present, and future. He said I was *special,* for the angels don't just appear to him when he gathers with people and hovers over them. So now I was wondering several things at this point. *He is crazy. I am crazy for talking with him, or we are both crazy because I, at this point in time, can't believe half of what he is telling me due to the fact that it is unbelievable.* Before he left that night, he said to me, "I am going to bless you by removing a layer of scales off of your eyes." I said to myself, "Sure, whatever that means." I had no idea that it meant my life would never be the same. He did this after warning me three times if I wanted to go down this path because I would never be the same. Oh, how true that statement became in my life. I have never been the same.

The next day, I rose up early to read my Bible since I was looking forward to Sunday service and wanted to study a little. When I read and want to do some studying, I usually look up a topic or a specific word to study, and it takes quite a bit of time of searching before I get my sermon together or just learn something new about God's Word. Well, this day was different in so many ways. I read the Bible, and a word or verse usually jumps out at me, and I know I am on the right track and continue to search and discover different things about God. On this day, it was really strange. I was reading, and the whole sentence was jumping off the page at me like magic or some kind of unexplainable way that I had never experienced before. They not only jumped out at me, but I was understanding them as well. I turned to a different book in the Bible, and it continued to happen. Sentences kept jumping out at me, and I was understanding them like never before. I had read these scriptures many times before but not like this, where revelation was coming to me. I was in awe and amazement. The next time I talked to the prophet, I told him about what happened, and he blew me away with his answer. He told me he knew what happened because my spirit was so excited that it told his spirit and woke him up. And I said, "What?" He explained that my spirit visited his spirit. It was so excited that it woke him up! *Somebody here is losing it, me or him.* I wasn't really sure at the time. I was just happy as to what had happened to me. He went on to explain, that's what he meant when he removed the scales off my eyes. I am able to see things that were hidden in the Bible that most people can't see. I said to him, "You're crazy!" I just understood things for some strange reason today. What you're telling me can't be true. There is no way. Yet I still see thing to this day when I read the Bible.

CHAPTER 2

Returning Home

I came home still thinking about the trip and all the things the prophet said from this trip. I was to go to Trinidad to bless these people, and I was the one who was blessed, not by the people but by my encounter with a prophet.

I had so much on my mind coming home on the plane that I couldn't sleep. It was like my mind couldn't stop thinking about God and what just happened to me while I was down there. I was wondering why God had chosen to touch me. Why were my prayers answered? I was still in shock to say the least. As I continued to talk to this prophet of God, I asked him, "Why me?" He said God heard my prayers, and that's why I encountered the prophet, and he came into my life. I wanted to know the deep things of God, and I had asked for wisdom, knowledge, and understanding. I was the one who had caused this encounter! I asked him why is God finally answering my prayers since I had many unanswered prayers in the past. He said that it was time to raise me up, for God needed me for this time in the battle of good and evil. I had many questions for him, and we had many conversations about all kinds of topics that would have you closing this book right now if you aren't ready for the truth. I was told some things once I got back home that had me almost not believing in God anymore. I got to the point that I thought this could not be true what this prophet was telling me, yet I continued to ask questions and listened to him. He warned me three times that the rabbit hole was deep, and I would not rest. Well, he wasn't wrong about that in my life. I had been searching for the deeper things of life ever since then.

One question that came up that you might wonder about, because I did, was how he did know about my prayers and part of my life. I asked him this exact question, so hold on because this is gonna blow your mind if you aren't ready for some truth. He told me that he had a near-death experience when he was seventeen years old. He went up to heaven while on the operating table at the hospital. He described it to me and said heaven was so beautiful that he didn't want to come back, but he had to. He now is able to go back and forth into the spiritual realm anytime he wants, and he has daily conversations with angels, like we have with people here on earth. So back to the question: "How did you know thing about me and my prayers?" He explained, "Remember the day I came to the church and meet you for the first time?" I replied yes. "Well, I usually mess with people's minds just to have fun. I usually tell them something about themselves and then tell them, 'Don't you remember me?' Knowing full well that these people have never met him in his life." He says this is his way of having fun with his gifts. Anyways, he was gonna do that with me, and the angels told him, "Put your ego in your pocket because this an *anointed man of God!*" When he told me that, I asked who they were talking about, and he said me.

He wasn't allowed to be played with like others because I was chosen by God. I understand this statement, yet I still don't understand this statement. How can a little-known pastor be so important to God when he has all these pastors already mighty and well-known by the world with thousands of followers? He went along to explain that it is because of my pure heart and my humble spirit.

I said, "Don't all pastors have those qualities?" He said, "No. Not all pastors have that in their life." I was a little confused by that statement. I thought all pastors have that quality in their lives; that's why they became pastors. We have had many conversations about this topic as well that we will discuss later on in this book, but for now, not all pastors have pure hearts or humbled.

So he went on to explain that the Lord's Prayer is deeper than we know. Matthew 6:8–13 states the following:

> Do not be like them, for your
> Father knows what you need before you
> ask him.
> "This, then, is how you should pray:
> 'Our Father in heaven,
> hallowed be your name,
> your kingdom come,
> your will be done,
> on earth as it is in heaven.
> Give us today our daily bread.
> And forgive us our debts,
> as we also have forgiven our debtors.
> And lead us not into temptation,
> but deliver us from the evil one.'"

Jesus explained how to pray in this verse, yet we don't understand the full meaning of this verse. Let me explain this verse a little as it was taught by my encounter with the prophet. He explained to me that God knows what you need before you ask. I said that was amazing, but he knew because we agreed to what was gonna happen in our lives. I said, "What are you talking about? I don't understand your statement." He said, "Continue to read the verse, and you will see."

> Our Father who art in heaven,
> hallowed be your name,
> your kingdom come,
> your will be done,
> on earth as it is in heaven.

"Okay, explain what he is saying in these statements."

I said, "We are to pray to God, our Father, who's in heaven. His name is sacred because He is God. And then God's kingdom will come once again here on earth in the second coming. God's will be done here on earth to show His power to bless people and show He is still alive." And I said, "How did I do?"

He said, "I guess that's good at your level right now. But let me explain to you how I knew about you and your prayers." I said to proceed with his explanation. "He was you or me, and God and I signed a legal document in heaven to come down here on earth before I ever left heaven. We both agreed on this document, and then we are sent to earth to fulfill this document—our will. When we come down here to earth, we have our memory erased while we are developing in our mother's womb, and then we start life." He said, "I just went to heaven and read your will and talked to your angel." And that's how he found out all about me. He wasn't allowed to interfere with my life because of my will, but we could negotiate with God. And the will could have a variation to it.

At this point in time, just like you are thinking, this man was crazy. So I did some experimenting of my own. I had other people talk to him, and he did the same thing and blew their minds, yet he got to mess with them in the process, which he wasn't able to do with me. He still does mess with me a little by teasing my mind about many different topics.

CHAPTER 3

What and Who Are the Prophets in the Bible

Prophet defined by dictionary.com:

prophet [prof-it]

noun

1. a person who speaks for God or a deity, or by divine inspiration.
2. (in the Old Testament)
    a) a person chosen to speak for God and to guide the people of Israel: *Moses was the greatest of Old Testament prophets.*
    b) (*often initial capital letter*) one of the Major or Minor Prophets.
    c) one of a band of ecstatic visionaries claiming divine inspiration and, according to popular belief, possessing magical powers.
    d) a person who practices divination.
3. one of a class of persons in the early church, next in order after the apostles, recognized as inspired

to utter special revelations and predictions. 1 Cor.
12:28.

4. the Prophet, Muhammad, the founder of Islam.
5. a person regarded as, or claiming to be, an inspired
    teacher or leader.
6. a person who foretells or predicts what is to come.

So this is the definition of the word *prophet*. Now here
are some of the main prophets in the Old Testament. Among
the prophets of the Old Testament were Daniel, Elijah,
Isaiah, Jeremiah, Jonah, and Moses.

In Numbers 11, Moses said the people were complaining about only eating mana and wanted to eat meat, so the
spirit of the Lord told Moses that he would feed them quail
for the next month, so tell the people. And here is the evidence of what happened.

> But Moses replied, "Are you jealous
> for my sake? I wish that all the Lord's people were prophets and that the Lord would
> put his Spirit on them!" Then Moses and
> the elders of Israel returned to the camp.
> Now a wind went out from the
> Lord and drove quail in from the sea. It
> scattered them up to two cubits deep all
> around the camp, as far as a day's walk in
> any direction. All that day and night and
> all the next day the people went out and
> gathered quail. No one gathered less than
> ten homers. Then they spread them out
> all around the camp. (Num. 11:29–32)

God used Moses to let the people know what He was gonna do in the future to come. Moses was also able to demonstrate God's power through him. He was able to part the Red Sea. He spoke to Pharaoh and caused plagues to come upon his people. Some caused it to not rain for three years. Others were able to pray for people and then be gone instantly and appear in another location.

> When they came up out of the water, the Spirit of the Lord suddenly took Philip away, and the eunuch did not see him again, but went on his way rejoicing. Philip, however, appeared at Azotus and traveled about, preaching the gospel in all the towns until he reached Caesarea. (Acts 8:39–40)

So there is much that a prophet can do because he is called by God for these purposes. There are many more prophets in the Old and New Testament, but I will continue to show you how all these things are still alive and well in our society today. Then we must always ask ourselves, Could this really be true in our society? How could this be, since we really don't see this happening today? Or is it happening, and we are unaware of these things going on every day? We must remember that God is the same yesterday, today, and forevermore. Nothing has changed since the beginning of time, according to God's Word.

I will give you testimony and facts from many people to let you know that God is still alive and that His prophets still live today. We must understand that these prophets are gifts from God. We might have even come in contact with them and either not recognize them or completely thought this person was crazy because of what they were saying. Maybe you have come across these exact, same type of persons that I am talking about. Some may even think they are from the devil, and they are an evil spirit. If you study these prophets in the Old and New Testament, you will see that they were able to do extraordinary things that people wouldn't believe today. I am letting you know now that I am sure, most of you have either come across a prophet or at least an angel of God in your lifetime. I looked back on my life and know that many a times, I have encountered an angel of God. And now I have encountered a prophet of God, who revealed himself to me. I have, for some reason, been chosen to be *blessed by God!* I was told because that's what I prayed for in my prayers. So it is my duty to share my encounter with this prophet and how God has now consumed me almost each and every day of my life. I would like to provoke you to think for yourself and not to be programmed by society to believe everything without proof or evidence. Anybody can say anything, but can they back up what they say with proof and evidence so that there is no doubt, even when the things said or done are almost impossible to believe? I need to be able to know these things really happened in somebody's life for me to believe. A prophet is able to do these things and many more.

CHAPTER 4

I Need Evidence for Me to Believe

I am like most of you, readers, not willing to believe anything and everything people say now in the times we live in. I like to do my own research and investigation on different stories or topics. I want to know and understand the topic we are discussing so I can make an informed decision. I don't want to look like a fool by repeating hearsay.

When I came back from my mission trip, my head was spinning, yet I wanted to believe God and the words he was speaking to me through my encounter with this prophet. I just couldn't believe the topics and the things he was telling me about the spiritual realm. It really made sense. But there was no evidence in the Bible to support his theories and of the stories he was telling me. So by all means, I was skeptical about these new revelations I was receiving. I now had spent twenty hours or so listening to him speak to me, and I was able to ask questions. But I still wasn't very sure about all that happened. I called to talk to him when I came back several times and got to know him even better. He gave me some advice on how to pray with my business partner, so I did. I just finished praying with him when the prophet called me. Is this a coincidence, or was the prophet watching in the spiritual realm and so happened to call once we finished praying? I let him talk to my business partner, and he did the exact same thing as he did to me when I was in Trinidad. He told him things about him that were spot-on because I asked him afterward about what was spoken about him, and he said they were spot-on. I thought to myself, *There is no way he could do this or even know this about my business partner. I mean, no way.* I was in awe after this conversation, as well as my business partner, and my mind was spinning. My business partner went home to follow the instructions the prophet gave him. And my wife was working late that day, so I wasn't worried or in a crunch time to stop talking to the prophet. I was still talking to the prophet when she came home. I introduced my wife to him on Messenger, and he proceeded to do the same thing with her. Now I was really blown away because we had been married for seventeen years, and he told her things that I was unaware of. And that was really scary. How could this prophet know these things about people who he has never met? I was blown away by how accurate he was and how easy it was for him to do so. He has done this to every person that I have introduced him to. I am still amazed at how easily he does this and how accurate he is every time he talks to people. How could this prophet know something so very deep about my wife that I didn't even know about? And I had been married to her for seventeen years. I was in disbelief! Talking about evidence; this was an understatement.

So by now, I have had one layer of scales removed from my eyes. I have had some deep mysteries of God's Word revealed to me, yet I still wanted more evidence that this prophet was from God and not the devil because I surely didn't want to be deceived. I was a believer of God and didn't want to go down a wrong path that would lead me to a place I didn't want to go—the evil side of this world. I told one of my daughters about this experience so she could share in the excitement I was experiencing. And let's say, she was less than impressed. She was sure I was heading down the wrong path that she contacted one of my closest friends and told him, "My dad needs help. He is talking nonsense and needs help. Could you please talk to him?" He called me, and we had a good talk. He said that I should talk to our pastor to see what he said about this matter. I proceeded to make an appointment to talk to our pastor, but it would take several weeks before he had some free time. I finally got to meet with him and explained to him that I met this person with special gifts, and I explained to him what happened to me while on my mission trip to Trinidad. He went on to explain that he had a couple of friends who he knew that had similar gifts. He explained that one lost his gift, and the other is doing good with his gift. But I should be careful and cautious about this guy. I told him that I would and thanked him for his time with me. After the meeting, I was feeling good about talking to the prophet and listening to all he was explaining to me about the wisdom and knowledge of the kingdom of God and how things in the spiritual realm work here on earth. (*More to come.*)

> The people were all so amazed that they asked each other, "What is this? A new teaching—and with authority! He even gives orders to impure spirits and they obey him." (Mark 1:27)

> Before I formed thee in the belly I knew thee; and before thou came forth

out of the womb I sanctified thee, and I ordained thee a prophet unto the nations. (Jer. 1:5)

I will raise them up a Prophet from among their brethren, like unto thee, and will put my words in his mouth; and he shall speak unto them all that I shall command him. (Deut. 18:18)

Jesus Made Fully Human

It is not to angels that he has subjected the world to come, about which we are speaking. But there is a place where someone has testified:
"What is mankind that you are mindful of them,
a son of man that you care for him?
You made them a little lower than the angels;
you crowned them with glory and honor
and put everything under their feet."
In putting everything under them, God left nothing that is not subject to them. Yet at present we do not see everything subject to them. (Psalms 8:4–6)

CHAPTER 5

The Power of Our Thoughts and Words

Repent at my rebuke!
Then I will pour out my thoughts to you,
I will make known to you my teachings.

—Prov. 1:23

The tongue has the power of life and death,
and those who love it will eat its fruit.

—Prov. 18:21

I was talking to the prophet one day, and we were talking about the kingdom of God and how things work in the spiritual realm. He asked me if I knew how things actually work. I told him my opinion, and I explained that by faith we pray to God, and then God answers prayers when the time is right, or he delays if we aren't ready for our prayers to be answered. He said, "I guess that's okay at milk level." He proceeded to explain to me that there are three levels of wisdom and revelation in the spiritual realm when we read and understand how things work and how deep certain things are explained in the Bible. He explained to me that many lessons and keys to the spiritual realm are taught in parables. Jesus mostly taught all the people and His disciples in parables. They would later discuss the parables in a different place or later on in different stories. He explained that these are "teaching hidden truths in plain sight." So let's get back to thoughts and words. Our thoughts are what we are wanting from God, and our words are our petition to God that coincide with our thoughts spoken out for the angels to take to heaven. Once the angels take these prayers to heaven, they are compared to our will to see if they need to be answered and returned to us as answered prayers. Sounds simple enough.

Well, let's say that wasn't quite correct, according to what the Word of God states.

> Jesus answered them, "Is it not written in your Law, 'I have said you are gods'?" (John 10:34)

> I said, "You are gods; you are all sons of the Most High." (Ps. 82:6)

He explained to me that we are able to create things in this world with our thoughts and words. I thought to myself, *This guy has lost his marbles, and maybe I have lost mine as well.* He proceeded to explain to me about my service the night he met me in Trinidad when I preached in Genesis how God created everything when He spoke. He explained to me the above verse and how I have the same power as my Father God. I am His child, therefore I can do some of the same things He is able to do once I understand the power that lies inside of me. We lost our memory when we came down to earth from heaven and have to be born again to understand and regain this knowledge. I wasn't too sure if I believed all of this, yet it made so much sense to me but seemed so far-fetched to believe. We talked and discussed this topic for a long time, and he said, "That's how you do things. You think about what you want, see it in your mind as happening in the future, then you speak it into existence." He proceeded to explain to me that you must believe what you speak and picture in your mind the results you want as though they have already happened.

I said, "It can't be that easy. I have a lot of things I had been praying for and have yet to see any results. I have a daughter who lives in Mississippi who I wanted to move to Texas so I could help her when she had any type of issues with her vehicle, money problems, or anything where I could help her." At this point in her life, I couldn't help her because she was so far away from me here in Houston, Texas. I thought this would be a good way for her to move here, and I could prove the prophet's theory to be true or all nonsense. I had asked my daughter to move here on many occasions, and she said, "I will never move to Texas!" I always explained to her that would be easier for me to help her and take care of her. Her answer never changed in all the times I asked her to come this way. Well, now was the chance to see if this ability to speak things into existence could really work. I prayed and saw her moving to Texas and felt good about it, except for where she was gonna stay. She was old enough to live on her own but still too young to understand how life really works. I thought maybe she could live with her mother, but then that wouldn't be to my advantage since we are not together anymore. I told myself I would sleep on it.

Well, life got busy, and I didn't think about it for several weeks since I wasn't sure where she could stay. Well, one day, out of the blue, my daughter calls and said, "Guess what, Dad, I'm moving to Texas!" I said, "Don't mess with me." She proceeded to say that she wasn't and that she would be moving in a couple of weeks. I was astonished at what I heard! My daughter was coming to Texas, just like I had prayed and visioned her. But I didn't even see in my prayer a place for her to stay. I guess the spiritual realm said they would find her a place, and it was with her mom, and I was okay with that. My heart, I think, skipped a beat when I heard this news for two reasons. First, I was getting my daughter back after many years of not being with her, so I was so ecstatic to have her back in my life. Second was that I was able to speak something into existence. I mean, how was that possible? I know my encounter with the prophet had some benefits, but to have my daughter back in my life was such a blessing to me that words can't truly tell the joy my heart felt at that moment! I thought of this as two miracles that happened to me, how God honored my words and changed my daughter's heart and mind to come to Texas. Second was that I spoke something into existence. My words created something out of nothing by using my words. It was truly amazing. What are the things I am realizing about the words that come out of my mouth? I have come to realize that *our words have power*, more power than we realize, the power to create or destroy things in our lives. Why we have the jobs we have, where we live, and even the vehicles we drive all come from this power we have inside of our mouths that we call words!

I have experimented on several occasions with the power of our words. Some of the things have come into existence, and others didn't. I was trying to call in crazy things, like purchasing lottery tickets and speaking that they were the winning tickets. Well, those words didn't come to pass, but you don't know if you don't try.

I do know that our words have tremendous power, and here are several stories to prove this particular point about the power that is within us. I work at a grocery store, and I am a department manager. There is a unit director of the store, and they have two store directors under them. Also there are two manager-in-charge (MICs) all under the authority of the unit director. Then we have about fourteen different department managers. Well, we were doing well as a store, but there were two department managers who were dragging down the spirits of the store with their horrible attitudes. Their department numbers, sales, labor spent, gross revenue that need to be obtained, keeping good people in their departments, etc. were all not good. I spoke into the spiritual realm that these two people needed to be gone from our store. I kept telling another manager and friend this for a while, and he agreed. Well, an amazing thing happened in the coming weeks. The one manager was fired or quit on his own. It didn't matter which one it was; what mattered was he is no longer in the store. The second manager was horrible because she treated her people so bad that many of her good people would quit! All she kept was the horrible workers because they had the same attitude she had. Well, they found out that she was doing some shady things, and she was fired. So I spoke into existence two people to leave the store, and it happened. Would you call this coincidence or the power of words? I will let you decide, but I know what I would call it.

I had another manager who would just get on people's nerves, and he was becoming a problem. I talked to the manager, who is a friend, and said two are gone. I thought we needed to get rid of this last one, so I spoke it into the atmosphere but a little different. He just had a child, and

I didn't want him to lose his job right after just having a baby. I requested that he just be transferred to another store. I had compassion on him since I saw what had happened to the other two managers. It wasn't that long when he came boasting to me how he was transferring to another store. I told him I already knew he was gonna transfer to another store. He said, "How did I know?" I went on to explain that it was me that caused him to transfer, and of course he didn't believe me. But I didn't care if he believed me or not; it was done. What I wanted to happen and spoke into the spiritual realm was in motion and that for him to transfer. You can think or try to convince yourself of what you want, but I am telling you facts of what happened. I was just as amazed as you are in reading about these things, especially when you read this for the first time.

CHAPTER 6

Jeremiah 33:3

Call to me and I will answer you and tell you great
and unsearchable things you do not know.

—Jer. 33:3

I had been talking to the prophet of God, and we had several deep conversations about angels and how the spiritual realm works. Well, I was explaining to the prophet that I was trying to contact my angel, and I was wanting to know how they would contact me back. The prophet said they do this in many ways; I just have to look and be aware of my surroundings. He said, sometimes they communicate through song, you'll see butterflies or rainbows, numbers will repeat themselves constantly, or even in scriptures they are communicating with us all the time. Once we established that we are aware of them in our lives, they are here to help guide and protect us through this journey called life.

I started to constantly talk to my angel when traveling to work since it is about a forty-five-minute drive. I told my angel that I was aware that he or she was there, and I wanted to communicate with them since they carry my prayers to heaven for me and executed them down here on earth. It started one day that I started to hear a couple of my favorite song, which lets me know that God was thinking about me, and He just wanted me know that He was here and hearing my prayers. I started to get really excited, knowing that I mattered to God. He was listening to my prayers and wanted me to be aware of this, so I knew God is real and wants to have a relationship with me while I am here on earth. I stared to see different sequences of numbers and took to the Internet to see the significance of these numbers. It stated out as the numbers 111. I got on YouTube and looked to see what it meant. Then 222 started popping up everywhere, so I knew I was on the right track.

Some of you are now probably thinking, *Oh, this is new-age teaching.* You call it what you want, but I call it communicating with the spiritual realm. It might be how it's called in our society, but I am telling you, in the spiritual realm, it's called communicating with your angel and God. Call it what you want, but this intimate conversation with my angel and God is so real that I couldn't deny what's going on in my life.

I then started to see the numbers 444, then 777, and looked up the meaning of these numbers. Next was 555, so I continued to look these numbers as well. I am not going to give you what they mean, for this would take too long. But if you do your own research, you will find out what they mean, and then you will see how it impacts your life and your journey in life. The last number sequence was 333. I was excited to continue to have my angel guide me and direct my path. But it seemed like so much work to gather all this information and figure it all out, so I decided to contact the prophet who I had an encounter with. He explained to me that maybe I should look up all the verses that had 3:33

or 33:3 in the Bible, and I might possibly find something. Well, to my surprise, I called the prophet, full of excitement and a mind-blowing revelation. I told him what I found in Jeremiah 33:3. He was shocked and amazed at what I discovered, looking so hard and finding this diamond in the Bible. He explained to me that I had been chosen for such a time as this and that it was to fulfill my purpose on earth.

> *Call to me and I will answer you and*
> *tell you great and unsearchable things you*
> *do not know.* (Jer. 33:3)

First, the prophet was amazed when I read him this scripture. He said he didn't even know that this particular scripture was even in the Bible and that I was able to find it. So I had shocked the prophet!

The prophet told me, that was part of the prayer that I prayed to God when he first met me, that I was praying for wisdom, knowledge, and understanding, that I would be able to have someone in my life to talk to about the deeper things of God. So let's break this verse down and see what it is actually saying. *"Call unto me."* Call unto God! I had been praying and calling unto Him, and my encounter with the prophet revealed that I had called. And he furthermore told me that I had given up so much in my life and had sacrificed so much that God heard me. He also said I had some much that had been taken away from me that God wanted to restore to me all that had been taken from me. He heard my prayers. Next is, *"I will answer you."* God said He would answer my prayers, which He has surely done all the way to this day that I am writing to you this book. On a side note, it was prophesied over me many years ago that I would write a book or two in my life. Wow, how spot-on is God in our lives. He does answer prayers and fulfill what He speaks into your life! Next is, *"He will show you great and unsearchable things."* So the question I had for God at this point when I first got this scripture is, How will I know it's true if it is unsearchable? How will I be able to explain your wonderful wisdom to your people, if people can't search it out? The things God has shown me aren't normal or average or even incredibly; they are great! You won't be able to explain it to people because it's unsearchable! This kind of wisdom, knowledge, and understanding only comes to the people seeking. I can't give you scriptures to back it up. I can't give you books from this world to look it up either. This is the mind-blowing things that come from the spiritual realm to those who seek. Scripture says:

> But if from there you seek the Lord
> your God, you will find him if you seek
> him with all your heart and with all your
> soul. (Deut. 4:29)

> I love those who love me, and those
> who seek me find me. (Prov. 8:17)

> Ask and it will be given to you; seek
> and you will find; knock and the door
> will be opened to you. (Matt. 7:7)

> God did this so that they would
> seek him and perhaps reach out for him
> and find him, though he is not far from
> any one of us. (Acts 17:27)

The last thing it says in the scripture is *"the things you do not know."* So these are new things because we don't know them. But how can you be taught great things, unsearchable things, and things you do not know? Why would God put something in the Bible that I am not able to search? These are some very important things to know and understand in your life before we can proceed. How do we find out this information if it's unavailable? Who is gonna know these things? As you can see, it brings up lots of questions, questions that some of you aren't ready for at this point in your life. I wasn't at first. I was almost devastated when I first started to hear all of this information. I started to believe God wasn't true or even existed when I first started this journey. I now know God is real!

I must warn you not to continue past this point in the book if you don't want to know the truth!

Stop for just a moment to collect your thoughts. You will need them if you want to continue on this journey. The truth isn't what you think it is.

> Then you will know the truth, and
> the truth will set you free. (John 8:32)

That was Jesus speaking in the above scripture. The truth will set you free, but it's not what you were taught in church. We were taught lots of good things in the church, yet this will be mind-blowing and will set you free from religion! What I am about to explain with you will go against a lot of what you were taught in churches all over the world. There is a difference between being a lamb in a flock and a lion in the jungle. The lamb follows the shepherd because he has no defenses; he can't protect himself. The lion, on the other hand, is the king of the jungle! He doesn't fear anything in the jungle. He rules the place in the jungle. He does the hunting. He is the king of the jungle! We have been trained and taught to be sheep instead of lions. We must change our thinking and be able to think and be rulers of our environment, not just followers of pastors because they guide us.

I know there are a lot of people seeking the truth in their lives. You know, there is more to God then you have been taught. You want to know the deeper things of God just like I did? Well, you are reading the right book to gain this insight for your life. You are getting ready to learn some of the keys to the kingdom of God if you choose to continue to read this book. But I must warn you again, don't go past this point if you aren't ready to know and understand the truth about God and His mysteries. I am telling you that what we have been taught in our churches isn't the deeper things of God but the kindergarten teaching of God!

Now you are either getting really excited to continue, or you are getting really upset with me right now with that previous statement. I am not sure which. But if you are in the second group, don't continue because you won't ever be the same. This is the second warning that I must give you before I continue with this book.

There is a movie series out that that explains this spiritual realm very well, it's called *The Matrix*. There is a scene in the first movie that the main character, Neo, is wanting to know the truth and is seeking it out, but he hasn't found it. He thinks he's being deceived in life by some system but can't quite put his finger on it. He is led to follow the white rabbit to a certain location, where he meets a lady named Trinity. She tells him, "I understand you want to know the truth," and he is stunned and wonders how she knows. She introduces him to a character named Morpheus. Morpheus, in a few scenes later, takes him to a room with two chairs and shows him two pills, a red pill and a blue pill. One will take him back to where he came from, and his life will be the same, and he won't remember anything. The other pill will take him down the rabbit hole of the truth, but he will never be able to return to his normal life again.

Well, my friends, you are now at the very same point in the movie. If you continue to read, your life will never be the same. You will be disconnected from what you thought was the truth into this new reality. So now you have been warned three times not to continue unless you want to go down this rabbit hole. Your mind will never rest, and you will seek more than you have ever thought possible in your life. Your world will be turned upside down, but the truth will set you free. I don't know what plans God has for you, but I know mine are to help others know the truth! If you are happy with your life now and don't have any problems in life, don't continue. Only continue if you are truly seeking because you will never rest again once you go down this rabbit hole of information. You have never heard of some of this information I am about to share with you. And you will have no way of disputing this information because you will have proof in your life that what I am telling you will come to pass. You will learn how things actually happen in the spiritual realm and the laws that govern our universe. The only way you can know this knowledge is to die and come back to earth or have a personal relationship with a man or woman of God themselves. This would be like Adam in the garden or Enoch, who was taken in a whirlwind; Moses talking to God in a bush. An experience like that is the other way.

So if we were gonna study something we know nothing about, we could get a book and start studying this topic and start to understand the topic. We could get on the Internet. We could google things and see what is known about this topic. We could talk to experts and see their points of view on the topics. And we could talk to people who oppose these theories to see if the topic is a fraud and unworthy of exploring any further. Once we learn about the topic, we would put into practice what we learned to see whose point of view is correct with proof and evidence!

So how do we start with the case of unsearchable and hidden things of God?

CHAPTER 7

❧

A Deeper Understanding
of the Mysteries of God

If you are reading this chapter, you must be really seeking the truth, or you are wanting to prove me wrong by seeing what nonsense I am talking about. Well, once you continue to read this book, your life is never going to be the same because your mind will be expanded, and you will never stop seeking God. And let me tell you this before we go on, you can't understand everything about God due to the fact that our little brains can't comprehend everything about God!

> "For my thoughts are not your
> thoughts, neither are your ways my
> ways," declares the Lord. (Isa. 55:8)

So I had all these questions about Jeremiah 33:3 that raced through my mind. How am I gonna learn all this stuff if it is unsearchable and hidden? These things that are not known, God, how will I find them? My encounter with the prophet was getting ready to go to another level. We were

37

gonna start talking and learning only what my mind could handle at this point in time. It's like anything you learn. You must start with the basic and then build upon those basics before moving on to the more challenging things. So we will start from the basics. My pastor said that there are three levels to the Bible: the surface level, the deeper level, and the revelation of the verse. What God is really trying to tell us? This is very true, and the prophet of God says it this way: milk level, meat level, and bone level. So there are three levels to the Word of God!

Most of the world is studying *milk level* because we are happy at this level. And since we are happy, we don't try to find the deeper things of God. When we go back in time, many thousands of years ago, people were taught in stories or parables. Traditions were passed on from generations to the next. They studied astronomy and had certain times of the year where they celebrated feast. They encountered things back then that we still try to understand today with all of our technology, such as the pyramids in Egypt and all across the world, all the writings across the world in some languages we still don't understand. We had many more books in the Bible that were taken out of the Bible, and some of the ones that are in the Bible aren't totally complete. An example of this is the book of Enoch. This is the person who was so intimate with God that God didn't let him die. So one must think, we should know more than a couple of verses about his life if his life was a wonderful example of how to live your life for God. Why would this book be eliminated from the Bible because it exists? There are several other books, such as the book of Judas, Gospel of Philip, Gospel of Mary, and many more. I have said all of this to show you we can't teach what we don't know. Christians have been taught only what has been taught for a few generations, and this goes back way past what we know and understand. We don't understand the spiritual realm at all or the power of God at all. We just have a slight understanding of how this works, but it's really not at all what you think it is to be plain and simple about it. We wonder why God isn't performing miracles like He used to in the Bible. Well, it is because we lack knowledge. We speak or talk a good talk, but we don't have any actions to support our beliefs. We say things like

> I am the gate; whoever enters through me will be saved. They will come in and go out, and find pasture. (John 10:9)

This was Jesus speaking. What are we saved from? When you ask a pastor what we are saved from, they will give you their answer. What are we saved from? Some say from hell. Some say from sin, and some say this will get you into heaven.

We will get more in-depth to the answer later on. We also claim this scripture in our lives.

> I can do all things through him who gives me strength. (Phil. 4:13)

> You, dear children, are from God and have overcome them, because the one who is in you is greater than the one who is in the world. They are from the world and therefore speak from the viewpoint of the world, and the world listens to them. We are from God, and whoever knows God listens to us; but whoever

> is not from God does not listen to us.
> This is how we recognize the Spirit of
> truth and the spirit of falsehood. (1 John
> 4:4–6)

We all hear and claim these wonderful words of God upon our lives, yet many, if not most, of us still live well below where God intends us to live. Why?

We go to church and listen to wonderful and inspirational sermons, yet we are not being taught how to activate the spiritual realm into our lives. Nobody is speaking about or even knowing anything about this untapped power of God that is at our disposal. Where are all the miracles from the Bible in today's society? Like when Peter's shadow came across people, they were healed—where are all these miracles?

> Very truly I tell you, whoever
> believes in me will do the works I have
> been doing, and they will do even greater
> things than these, because I am going to
> the Father. And I will do whatever you
> ask in my name, so that the Father may
> be glorified in the Son. You may ask me
> for anything in my name, and I will do it.
> (John 14:12–14)

I haven't seen anybody break bread and fish and feed thousands. I haven't seen anybody walk on water. I haven't seen anybody heal people like Jesus did or cast out spirits and demons. I haven't seen anybody command the storms to cease, and the storms did cease. Where is all this if God spoke it in the verses above?

Or is it being done, and we are unaware of this going on in the world today? We will be getting to this later in the book. We live in a society that only wants milk level because people are happy at this level. Some seek a deeper level and never find it. I am not sure why, but I have been blessed to have been chosen to go to the next level. God has chosen me to share things with you, the reader, that will change your way of thinking and might even get you to believe that there is a God! I am not here to change your beliefs or religion. I am here to explain to you some spiritual concepts to help you in life if you are willing to listen and open your mind to these things. What do you have to lose but maybe some time in your life to complete this book and practice what you are reading? Unless your life is at a point of fullness that you just can't have any more blessings in your life and the truth to obtaining blessings in your life, then maybe this book isn't for you. Maybe I am just a madman like you believed when you first started reading this book. But what if there is more to life than what you thought? What if everything you believed in was wrong? Could this be the book for you? Could your life be better than it has ever been? I will be sharing some truths about the spiritual realm that will blow your mind. You might even think that it's a lie or from the pits of hell, but I assure you, it's just the opposite. All that I will be sharing with you is straight from heaven and the spiritual realm.

> "For my thoughts are not your thoughts, neither are your ways my ways," declares the Lord. (Isa. 55:8)

So as you can see from the verse above, your thoughts are not God's thoughts. Or we can say, it is not His way of thinking. Your ways of doing things isn't God's way of doing things. I don't know how different it is, a little different or extremely different. But I am guessing the second, extremely different, which means that everything I am writing has a possibility of being exactly how God does things because it goes against everything you think and do in life! Now that's a powerful statement! Ponder on that for a while, and let that really soak into your thinking! The way you have been living your life could be totally different than the way God thinks and acts! I fall into that category. I thought I was doing everything the way God wanted me to live, just to come to find out I knew nothing at all! All the things I thought I knew was nothing at all. I had no clue as to what and how God acted at all. I was clueless as to how the spiritual realm worked. I didn't know that everything I needed to accomplish anything was already inside of me, I just wasn't aware of this or the process on how to tap into this knowledge.

> The kingdom of heaven is like treasure hidden in a field. When a man found it, he hid it again, and then in his joy went and sold all he had and bought that field. (Matt. 13:44)

I was told this scripture many a times and have come to understand its meaning. The treasure is knowing *the truth!* This statement is worth the purchase of this book. Knowing the truth will help set you free, then you will get a deeper level of understanding of God. To understand God's Word is to understand God's mysteries "hidden in plain sight." I was amazed at what happened in my life and the joy it brought to my life when a layer of scales were removed from my eyes. I was able to read God's Word, and the hidden mysteries jumped out at me, along with the revelation of that verse. If I didn't understand the verse, I was able to discuss it with the prophet, and he would guide me into revelation or direct me where to find the answer. I was then able to tap into the spiritual realm and its power. I am still far away from where I want to be, but I am growing daily and know one day I will get to where I want to be.

Now I want you to understand that there are people who will never see what I see or believe what I believe, and I am all right with that. You must understand that unless God chooses to open your eyes to certain things, you will never see it! It's just that simple. And I can't change that for your life. I would read things and then have my wife read the same verse of scripture, and she would get nothing from that scripture. I would be dumbfounded because it was right there in plain sight. I would also have my son read the exact same scripture, and he would be the same as my wife. I would think and say to myself, "Why can't they see and understand that scripture? What is wrong with them?" I was then told, not everyone can see what I see. I would go on to explain that verse, and they couldn't understand the verse right after I just explained it to them. They couldn't see what I see or understand what I could understand. It was hidden from them, but I hope to be able to explain it to them until they can understand, and I hope they can understand scriptures like I do.

Remember when Jesus died and rose again from the tomb, two angels appeared to Mary and said, "Who do you seek?" She told them, "My Lord, they have taken the body." Then she looked outside of the tomb and thought she was talking to the gardener. But it was really Jesus. Jesus had hidden himself from Mary.

Another story is this:

Now that same day two of them
were going to a village called Emmaus,

> about seven miles from Jerusalem. They were talking with each other about everything that had happened. As they talked and discussed these things with each other, Jesus himself came up and walked along with them; but they were kept from recognizing him. (Luke 24:13–16)

Jesus kept them from recognizing Him. More on this in later chapters. God can keep you from recognizing Him in His word as well as in person. He can keep things hidden from whoever He chooses. So now I understand why my wife and son were unable to understand what I was trying to share with them. Some or most of you will be in the same boat as them, so I won't be disappointed about your comments when you are done reading this book. Others will see life in a totally new way and start down this path of wonder and amazement. You will be able to see this truth and will never be the same.

CHAPTER 8

K + V = M

This is a very interesting and powerful formula. I will explain this formula here in a minute, but I want you to know that I and many others have used this formula successfully. I will explain the formula and give you examples of how this works. So let's get started on this adventure.

K stands for knowledge. V stands for vision. M stands for manifestation. So *knowledge + vision = manifestation*.

We must know how knowledge is used to tap into this powerful statement.

> My people are destroyed from lack of knowledge.
> Because you have rejected knowledge, I also reject you as my priests; because you have ignored the law of your God, I also will ignore your children.
> (Hosea 4:6)

We must have knowledge on how things work in the spiritual realm. We must know how to obtain this knowledge. We must believe that what we pray is going to happen. We can't doubt that our prayers will be answered.

> Jesus replied, "Truly I tell you, if you have faith and do not doubt, not only can you do what was done to the fig tree, but also you can say to this mountain, 'Go, throw yourself into the sea,' and it will be done." (Matt. 21:21)

In this passage of Scripture, we see the power that lives inside of Jesus. He spoke to the fig tree, and it died because it wasn't bearing fruit, which a fig tree should bear figs. The fig tree wasn't doing what it was designed to do, produce figs for consumption. So the question is, are we producing what we are designed to produce? Are we feeding the people of this world with what they need to consume in life? Are we helping them with being successful in life? There are a lot of interesting questions we need to answer in our lives.

There is also another point to this passage that we must understand that is *very important!* We all understand that Jesus was the Son of God and is able to tap into the spiritual realm. The word of God tells us that we are the children of God and sons of God. So that means that we have some of the same characteristics of God, after all we were created in His image and likeness. I noticed that when I look at my children, they have some of my qualities. They look like me. Some have an attitude like mine. Some think like me. Some like the same hobbies as mine, and I could go on. The point I am trying to make is, they have some of my exact qualities. Well, when God created us, it's the same. We have some of the *same, exact qualities of God!* This may blow your mind, but you have God's qualities inside of you, and you probably didn't even know it. You have the ability to speak to things, and they happen in your life. I know some of you are saying to yourself, "I prayed for someone to be healed, and God didn't answer my prayers." You might have prayed over finances, healings, relationships, etc., and they didn't happened, or had any number of things that you prayed over, and they didn't happen, I know I was in the same boat. I prayed over many things, and nothing happened. I get it! Now I have become more educated in the knowledge of God, and things are changing in my life. Now, with this knowledge, I don't pray like I used to. I pray, knowing things will happen and not hoping things will happen! There is a big difference in these two statements. Before, I hoped things would happen, and now, I know and project this on my prayers and requests to God! When I speak, I know God is going to move in the spiritual realm for me because I see my prayers answered before they ever occur in my life. I don't continue to pray the same thing over and over either. The reason being is because God isn't deaf! He hears our prayers before we even pray them and, for sure, when we speak them. So when you continue to pray the same thing, it means you doubt! You are doubting that God heard you or that He is acting on your behalf.

There is an enemy out there that sometimes is keeping your prayers from coming down here to earth, but they are fighting to get here. They sometimes just need help getting to you.

Then he continued, "Do not be afraid, Daniel. Since the first day that you set your mind to gain understanding and to humble yourself before your God, your words were heard, and I have come in response to them. But the prince

of the Persian kingdom resisted me twen-
ty-one days. Then Michael, one of the
chief princes, came to help me, because
I was detained there with the king of
Persia. Now I have come to explain to
you what will happen to your people in
the future, for the vision concerns a time
yet to come." (Dan. 10:12–14)

We need to know that God hears us. But we must also
know, there is an enemy out there fighting in the spiritual
realm to hinder our prayers. Believe that you receive when
you ask!

But when you ask, you must believe
and not doubt, because the one who
doubts is like a wave of the sea, blown
and tossed by the wind. (James 1:6)

When we don't understand what is happening in the
spiritual realm, we doubt that God is doing anything. So as
the above scripture states, we are like waves of the sea, blown
and tossed by the wind. *We have power when we speak*; we just
don't realize this or even believe this statement! We think we
can say whatever we want and that there are no consequences
for what we say! Wrong! Those words that come from our
mouths are the weapons that can change your life forever.
They take you where you want to go or down the wrong path
of life. When you speak to your spouse or children, you are
speaking life or death to them. You are either building them
up or tearing them down; it's your choice. But once those
words come out of your mouth, they are affecting the spiritual realm. You have sent them out into the universe where

God is at, and He is sending His angels to perform what you are speaking, no matter how good or bad. An example of this is when you say, "I can do this, whatever it is," and you do it, or you say, "I can't do that, whatever that is," and you aren't able to perform the task. You are calling things into existence! You believe the statement you made, so your subconscious tells itself you can or can't do what you just said. You totally believe it, so it happens! You cause it to happen and believe it to be real in your life. When Jesus spoke to the fig tree, He spoke to it knowing it would happen. He believed it in His subconscious that what He said was true and that it would die because He spoke it and believed it to be. We can do the same things in our lives. Now I know what you're thinking. We aren't Jesus! You are correct to think that, but you have the same abilities. I know you are saying, "This man is crazy! He is out of his mind. Maybe it was a mistake to even pick up this book." Hold on. Let me show you what I am saying it true, 100 percent!

> Very truly I tell you, whoever believes in me will do the works I have been doing, and they will do even greater things than these, because I am going to the Father. (John 14:12)

So there is your proof that what I am saying it true! That was Jesus making that statement, not me making up something for this book. The word is either all true or all lies. You either believe all of what God says or don't believe any of it at all. We have been led to believe that it is a good story, but we can't do what the word says. I can't call things into existence; that's impossible! Or is it possible? You'll have to continue to read as I prove this point to you.

Let me give you a tremendous miracle that happened when my wife and I tried this theory. On a Friday evening, our daughter called my wife with a pain in her voice, and we didn't know why but knew that something was wrong. She spoke to my wife for quite a long time. When she hung up from the phone conversation and explained to me what was going on, she said that her husband's boss was on life support, and the family was having to make a difficult decision and wanted us to pray that the family would make the right decision. The family had two options to choose from. First was to take him off life support, and he would most likely be in a vegetative state the rest of his life, or the second choice was that if they pulled the plug, he would pass. Not very much of a choice if you ask me and my wife. We said, "Why don't we put into practice a different option? Why don't we pray for a total healing?" We agreed that this was the best option of all. We prayed and saw him totally healed and whole the way we were designed by God. We stood in the gap for the family, but we spoke something in the spiritual realm that we knew would happen if we could see it in the natural. Well, a couple days went by, and we didn't hear anything from our daughter. So we decided to call her and see what his status was since we called certain things into existence. She said she was scared to call because she didn't know if the news was bad or good. We told her to call and follow up on his status. She called my wife with disbelief! She couldn't believe what had happen. They explained to her that when they pulled the plug of his life support, he woke up! What, he woke up? Yes. And he wasn't in a vegetative state or died. He recognized everything and everybody in the room. What a miracle! God performed everything that we requested and spoke into existence. The boss is currently at work and doing fine. He is a walking miracle and nothing less. So you see, we can speak things into existence.

Don't let anyone tell you anything different. You can speak things into existence. That's God's word. I just followed the knowledge that I obtained from God and my encounter with the prophet.

> While he was saying this, a synagogue leader came and knelt before him and said, "My daughter has just died. But come and put your hand on her, and she will live." Jesus got up and went with him, and so did his disciples.
>
> Just then a woman who had been subject to bleeding for twelve years came up behind him and touched the edge of his cloak. *She said to herself, "If I only touch his cloak, I will be healed."*
>
> Jesus turned and saw her. "Take heart, daughter," he said, "*your faith has healed you.*" And the woman was healed at that moment. (Matt. 9:18–22)

So the question to ask is, how was she healed? Did Jesus heal her, or did she heal herself because of what she believed? Jesus said, "Who touched me?" because virtue or power came out of him. Why? What caused that to happen? The woman believed that if she touched him, she would be healed. Her faith or belief in this action caused heaven to move and her healing to be received. Some of you are saying, "But she touched the Son of God, that is why she was healed." True! But Jesus said "who touched me?" because He didn't have anything to do with her healing. Many people were touching

Jesus at that time. They were bumping into Him, trying to reach Him and hear Him speak or see miracles happen in people's lives. On this occasion, a woman with a problem or condition touched Him with a belief. She touched Him with a purpose! She wanted to gain something from the touch, her healing. She caused the virtue or power to be released from Jesus. He didn't do anything to cause this to happen. He was walking to another location to help somebody else when this occurred. Her thought or belief that was created in her mind caused something in the spiritual realm to happen. Jesus was the point of contact for this to happen. But why then were other people not healed that we're bumping into Jesus? They didn't expect something to happen like the lady did. She caused the miracles to happen. So then, why aren't we making things happen in our world? Are we not expecting the virtue of God to happen? Is our faith or belief not the same as this lady's? We must be doing something wrong in the process. We are children of God, so we should have virtue come from us when we touch others or when someone touches us. What is this story with the lady with the issue of blood telling us? Could it be of some importance to this simple story? The impact of our faith and belief, as well as what we focus on when we pray and believe. She was focused on touching Jesus and then receiving her healing. We must press into the spiritual realm in order to receive from the spiritual realm.

Another thing of importance is her emotions. We know that she had this issue for twelve years, and it must have been draining to her emotions. It had already drained her finances because she had money; the Bible tells us. We must think and realize that this issue in her life had an emotional effect on her as well. She tried everything the doctors at that time knew to do to help her. Nothing helped her. She heard that Jesus was able to heal people and that He was there in her town. She, according to the law of her day, wasn't even allowed in town, or she could be put to death because of the condition she was in with her sickness. She didn't care about that because she was dying. What was going on in her thoughts or mind at that time? *I am gonna die if I don't attempt to receive my healing. Or if I stay outside of town, I will surely die with no help.* Her heart must have been pounding as she made her way to attempt to touch Jesus. *What if somebody sees me before I make it to Him? Will I be stoned to death before I can attempt to touch Him? I must try. Because if they recognize me, I will die and not have to suffer anymore.* The only problem with that is her hope and faith that she would be healed outweighed her fear! She had nothing to lose and everything to gain. Her emotions cancelled her fear! She attempted to touch Him so she would have a chance of being healed. "I might be healed if I touched Him" would mean there was doubt. She had none of that when she made this decision to touch Him. She was 100 percent expecting to receive her healing upon touching His garment. Her emotions were tied to her faith and expectations. She saw herself healed upon touching His garment. Let me say that again, because I think you missed that statement. She saw herself healed when she touched His garment, which means, she activated healing. She caused her own healing. Her mind chose to believe that touching Jesus would heal her, and it did exactly what she believed. Jesus wanted to know who tapped into heaven and the spiritual realm became virtue or power just left His body.

Once you learn about the power that lies within you, you will be able to tap into this same power as well. Knowledge is power! The world doesn't want you to know this, and most pastors don't know about tapping into the spiritual realm. Hence that is why the church doesn't teach this because you can't teach what you don't know. They will use this example to inspire you to believe and to build up your faith. They just can't reproduce this example in real life. And if they do, it won't be done on a consistent basis. They will have somebody healed here and there, but not all people will be healed. If we all can't be healed, why tell this story? Does God only love certain people? And if you aren't loved, then you can't be healed. That doesn't sound right. I though He was a loving God, a just God who cared for His people, a God of compassion. Knowledge is the key factor here. And if you don't know certain things that happen in the spiritual realm, you won't be able to have your healing.

With my encounter with the prophet, he uses a scripture to teach me about knowledge. Here is the scripture below:

The Parables of the Hidden Treasure and the Pearl

> The kingdom of heaven is like treasure hidden in a field. When a man found it, he hid it again, and then in his joy went and sold all he had and bought that field. (Matt. 13:44)

Knowledge is the treasure in the field. The knowledge of the spiritual realm is so vast; it has taken me a long time to understand it and how it works. I am still learning on a daily basis. But once you understand, the value is of tremendous effect in your life. You have now tapped into the *power of God*!

CHAPTER 9

Sin

This chapter is going to open a lot of eyes that I hope you are ready to receive, or you might be discouraged. Here we are gonna learn a couple of things that will really get your mind spinning if it isn't already.

To start, let us describe what sin is.

Sin

1.
    a)   an offense against religious or moral law

    b)   an action that is or is felt to be highly reprehensible

It's a *sin* to waste food.

    c)   an often serious shortcoming: FAULT

2.
    a)   transgression of the law of God

    b)   a vitiated state of human nature in which the self is estranged from God

verb
sinned; sinning
Definition of sin (Entry 2 of 4)
intransitive verb

1.   to commit a sin
2.   to commit an offense or fault

Vitiated
Definition of vitiate
transitive verb

1.   to make faulty or defective: IMPAIR

The comic impact is *vitiated* by obvious haste.
— William Styron

2.   to debase in moral or aesthetic status

a mind *vitiated* by prejudice

3.   to make ineffective

Fraud *vitiates* a contract.

Another way to define sin is "missing the mark." When God asks us to do something, whatever it might be, and we don't do it, we sin. It could be as easy as a thought that comes into my head, like, *hey, I should purchase some flowers for my wife before I come home*, and I didn't do it, I miss the mark. I didn't do what God is asking me to do.

We also assume it to be something like adultery, stealing, murder, hate, or something along those lines, these are sins as well. But anytime we don't do what God is asking us to do or break a law that He said we should follow, we sin. We miss the mark set by God for our lives to follow. We must come back to the start and try again. The next day or that same day, I must go and purchase those flowers for my wife. It's not to earn brownie points, but she might be going through something that day that I don't know about. She needs those flowers to show love or appreciation for what she went through. And if she didn't go through anything, she needs to know she is loved! Either way, God wants her to have those flowers, and He has a reason for them in her life. I just need to follow His instructions.

When we miss the mark, God still loves us, and we are still His children who He loves no matter what. What we are trying to do is not miss the mark so much. We are walking daily, trying to hit the mark, trying to hone our skills on hearing Him speak and doing His will in our lives.

> Jesus stepped into a boat, crossed over and came to his own town. Some men brought to him a paralyzed man, lying on a mat. When Jesus saw their faith, he said to the man, "Take heart, son; your sins are forgiven."
>
> At this, some of the teachers of the law said to themselves, "This fellow is blaspheming!"
>
> Knowing their thoughts, Jesus said, "Why do you entertain evil thoughts in your hearts? Which is easier: to say, 'Your sins are forgiven,' or to say, 'Get up and walk'? But I want you to know that the Son of Man has authority on earth to

forgive sins." So he said to the paralyzed man, "Get up, take your mat and go home." Then the man got up and went home. When the crowd saw this, they were filled with awe; and they praised God, who had given such authority to man. (Matt. 9:1–8)

In this story, Jesus forgave the man's sin before he did anything else. Why? Why would Jesus do something like this if there wasn't a message in this story hidden in plain sight? When we have our sins forgiven, we reset ourselves. We go back to our original state, as if we never sinned. We go back to the way God created us in the beginning of time, perfect in all our ways. We get a redo. We start all over again, perfect in his eyes. God is perfect, and only perfection is allowed in heaven. We get that same perfection when we have our sins forgiven. We are reset into that perfect state that our bodies so eagerly desire to be in, and we search for this state all the days of our lives. And some of you don't even know it or why we search. It's in our DNA! We want to know about our Creator and long to go back to perfection. We sometimes live our whole lives wondering about life and searching for its meaning because we miss that state of perfection where we first came from. So once our sins are forgiven, we go back to the reset position, and this is very important. With sin still inside of us, we are not in a perfect state when we desire our healing. We are impure with sin in our lives. Remember, we are trying to tap into the spiritual realm, and there are certain laws that must be followed for things to happen. So when Jesus said, "Your sins are forgiven," He reset the man's life to be healed. He was now in a perfect state to be healed. He was prepared for his miracle to happen now that he was in a perfect state in the spiritual realm. Then Jesus went on to heal him. You might not agree with this statement, but I assure you, things happen when we are reset in the spiritual realm.

My encounter with the prophet has shown me many things, and now I am going to tell you a story to help prove this story in modern times.

The prophet himself has chickens where he lives, and a dog came along and killed many of them. One day, the dog had come back, and the prophet was waiting on the dog. He took his gun and decided to shoot the dog for killing his chickens. He shot the dog that day, and the dog struggled down a way to a ditch and collapsed. Some of pastor's friends and church members were there and were sad the dog was shot. They went to see how the dog was doing and came back to report to the prophet how the dog was. They said the dog was shot in the back and couldn't walk anymore and would die because it could not get food or water anymore. They pleaded with the prophet to help the dog. At first, he didn't want to help because the dog had killed his chickens. He then felt bad for the people and the dog, so he said, "Your sins are forgiven." To the members' surprise, the dog got up and started to head toward the house. He started to come, limping, which then went away, and the dog was 100 percent healed with no limp or sign that it had been shot. He didn't pray for healing for the dog. He said, "Your sins have been forgiven." The dog was healed and now has become a pet for the family, running as if he had never been shot. How do you explain that? The prophet said, by forgiving his sins, the dog went back to his original state of perfection. In other words, before the dog was shot, it was healthy with no limp or injury. Well, that's what happened. The dog was healed.

We must understand these principles that work in the spiritual realm and how they work in order to tap into their power. Not all things are what we think they are. This story shows us the power of forgiveness, the power of restoration.

Here is another example of forgiveness, which I experienced in my own life. We have several men's camps every year, and my children had unforgiveness for having affairs and causing my divorce from my first wife. They have had this unforgiveness for twenty-plus years. Well, I had the chance to invite one of my sons to this camp because he wanted to change his life and started to seek after God now. This camp was a four-day camp with only about fifteen to eighteen campers. We go through lots of videos and exercises so the campers could learn how to listen to and experience God for themselves. There was this one part where they asked for forgiveness of any of their sins so they could be healed from their past and start new. During this part of the exercise, I asked God if it would be better for me to step outside when my son spoke so my son could open up to the others and not have to worry about holding anything back. God said, "Sit down and listen to what your son has to say." I said, "Okay, I can do that." Boy, it was good for him to release all those years of hurt and pain, but for me, I was crushed and hurt. I know I caused all this pain, but to hear it directly from him in a group setting was very painful to me. I was later told how cruel and mean I was to put my family through so much pain and hurt. I felt about six inches tall after his story. But wait, it got much better. My son had to get on his knees and ask God to forgive him for holding on to all this hate and unforgiveness. As he was doing this, I was told to tell him I was sorry for causing all of this hurt and pain. We both cried and forgave each other. We held each other and were healed of all the pain and hurt in our lives. We were reset as father and son. And to this day, we spend time talking and laughing together because we were healed from our past.

There were many tears shed during that camp, and I will always cherish that moment when we forgave our past sins and restored our father-son relationship. I give God all the glory for that healing, and it came with forgiveness of sins! We were both able to forgive each other and be healed, just like the previous story. The restoration of our relationship is evident only because of forgiveness! Forgiveness healed our relationship, and we were able to move forward with our father-and-son relationship. We were able to restore or heal our relationship because of forgiveness of sin. This is such a powerful statement that most of us seem to overlook in our lives. When people hold on to those past hurts and pain, it will always hold them back from healing their lives. They will always suffer and struggle in life. They are missing the mark in not wanting to reset their lives to its original state. This is so critical for us to understand and be able to move forward. If we don't do this, we will get stuck in life and not grow but struggle through life.

CHAPTER 10

Angels and Favor

You have made them (man/woman)
a little lower than the angels
and crowned them with a *glory* and *honor.*

—Ps. 8:5

Definition of *glory*

1.

    a)   praise, honor, or distinction extended by common consent: RENOWN

    b)   worshipful praise, honor, and thanksgiving

giving *glory* to God

2.

    a)   something that secures praise or renown

the *glory* of a brilliant career

    b)   a distinguished quality or asset

The *glory* of the city is its Gothic cathedral.

3.
    a)   a state of great gratification or exaltation

When she's acting, she's in her *glory*.

    b)   a height of prosperity or achievement

ancient Rome in its *glory*

4.
    a)
        1)   great beauty and splendor: MAGNIFI-
            CENCE

…the *glory* that was Greece and the grandeur that was
Rome.
— E. A. Poe

        2)   something marked by beauty or resplen-
            dence

a perfect *glory* of a day

    b)   the splendor and beatific happiness of heaven

broadly: ETERNITY

5.   a ring or spot of light: such as
    a)   AUREOLE
    b)   a halo appearing around the shadow of an object

Definition of *honor*

1.
    a)   good name or public esteem: REPUTATION
    b)   a showing of usually merited respect: RECOG-
        NITION

pay *honor* to our founder

2.   PRIVILEGE

had the *honor* of joining the captain for dinner

3.   a person of superior standing—now used especially
     as a title for a holder of high office

if Your *Honor* please

4.   one whose worth brings respect or fame: CREDIT

an *honor* to the profession

This is how God made us, yet we don't see ourselves like this. We only tend to think of all the mistakes we have made in our lifetime and never really dwell on what God thinks about us! We never go and study God's point of view on the matter. We are too caught up on seeing things from Satan's point of view, the father of all lies. I was taught that there are always two points of view. There is God's point of view, and then there is Satan's point of view. We seem to always lean toward the second, instead of the first point of view. Why do we do this stupid thing and believe the lie? Why don't we believe what God says about us to be true and believable? Maybe because we have been brainwashed into not thinking that we are not worthy of God's point of view because of our past failures. We think, since we have failed so many times, that God couldn't think of us with glory and honor. We are not that worthy! We could never live up to that standard. We are just trying to survive most of the time and not overcoming our sins on a daily basis. God see us with sin and imperfection and still wants us to be crowned with glory and honor! I didn't write the Bible; I am just informing you of what it says. You need to know that the Creator of this world and the universe crowned you with glory and honor. Wow, now that's a powerful statement when you let that sink into your spirit. God is all-knowing and knows I fall short on a daily basis and still decides to crown me with glory and honor. I am so excited right now; I am screaming with excitement! I didn't have to try to obtain glory and honor; God predestined this to happen thousands of years ago for me right now! When He created everything that exists now, this is what God wanted me to know. God, You are so amazing.

You need to go back and read what God says about you when you feel down or discouraged. He is the one who gave you this crown while you live here on earth. Right now, you should take a few minutes to meditate on this passage and what God is trying to reveal to you at this point in time with your life. Some of you are going through some tough times, and this will inspire you to see life from a different perspective—God's perspective about you.

I have a good friend who explained to me, when you put a diamond under a light, all kinds of colors appear as you move the diamond at different angles of the light. From one point of view, the diamond might be blue, but from another point of view, it might be red. So which view is right or correct? They both are, because they see things from different perspectives or points of the diamond. So when we see our-selves as blue—for example, when feel bad not living up to what we think are God's expectations—God sees red in His point of view and sees you crowned with glory and honor, proud of you and full of love toward you. You are the apple of His eye. He speaks so magnificently of His creation. And that would be you, His creation.

> For he will command his angels
> concerning you to guard you in all your
> ways; (Ps. 91:11)

I can look throughout my life and see where God's angels have guarded my life on several occasions. I remember one time while driving back to college one night. It was about a five-hour drive, and I decided to drive back in the evening when it wasn't so hot, since my car back then didn't have AC. I left around five or six. And about two to three hours into my trip, I fell asleep while driving my car. All I remember was being on the other side of this two-lane highway in the grass when I woke up. I realized what happened and grabbed the wheel to get me back on my side of the highway. Once that occurred, my car stalled out. I could have easily hit a car if one was coming or hit the grass on the other side and flipped my car and crashed. I believe angels were around my car, protect-ing me and my car from any harm. After realizing the total picture of what just happen, I didn't fall asleep the rest of that trip. I know my angels were watching over me that night.

On another occasion, I was working later in life in the restaurant business and was closing the store that night. After work, some of the employees and myself were drinking, and I had a little too much to drink. I thought I could make it home from work. The drive was only like thirty minutes away. Well, there was construction on the freeway on the other side of this newly constructed bridge. They had barrels along the route to guide you where to go and block of where not to go. Once I crossed the bridge, I must have lost focus since I passed between two barrels and didn't hit either one of them and made it home safe that night. I am not saying to go out and drink and do stupid things like that. I am saying, even though I did stupid things, God still had His angels protect me.

Nowadays, I have angels on my side, protecting me from police speed traps. When I go by them, there are two things that happen. First, and the most common of the two, is that the speed trap is on the other side of the freeway. I don't have to worry about it at all. Or second, they are on my side, and it's like they don't see me or are distracted when I come by where they are posted. I know this because one time I was at least going fifteen miles over the speed limit and just knew that cop's lights would be on me, but there was nothing. I proceeded to thank my angel for protecting me from any harm to my pocketbook. So these are just a few examples from my life. I am sure you have some examples from your life if you look back and reflect.

> I tell you, whoever publicly acknowledges me before others, the Son of Man will also acknowledge before the angels of God. (Luke 12:8)

This is such a powerful statement. Do you realize that Jesus is in heaven right now on your behalf, letting angels know about you and giving them charge over your life as you read? He said, "Acknowledge me before others, and I will acknowledge you before the angels of God." God is letting angels know about you and then assigning them *task* on your behalf. He is letting the angels know and understand your importance to His kingdom. He is willing to take care of you and protect you with the angels at His command. You are very important to God. He is doing everything on His part to guide you and lead you to the ways of truth. He has angels at our side to protect us and intervene in our lives, so He gets all the glory. He wants the world to understand how much He loves us and cares for us. If you know the power angels have over our lives, you would be astonished. They are the ones who fulfill God's commands. They get things done here on earth. They can come to your rescue when you're in times of danger and can calm the fear in your life with their presence. On that note, when they appeared in the Bible, some of their first words were "fear not." They can set fear into people as well. But since we are on God's side, we fear not.

They were assigned to Daniel in the lions' den to protect him from the sure death from the lions. He not only survived this situation, but on the next day, the king threw his accusers into the lions' den, and they didn't fare as well. They became the lions' food for that day.

When we are acknowledged before the angels of God, we have access to the power of God. These are the ones who fulfill the commands of God. They can either help you or come to take you.

Angels have come to earth to sometimes take out our enemies. They have done this on many occasions.

> When the servant of the man of God got up and went out early the next morning, an army with horses and chariots had surrounded the city. "Oh no, my lord! What shall we do?" the servant asked.

"Don't be afraid," the prophet answered. "Those who are with us are more than those who are with them."

And Elisha prayed, "Open his eyes, Lord, so that he may see." Then the Lord opened the servant's eyes, and he looked and saw the hills full of horses and chariots of fire all around Elisha.

As the enemy came down toward him, Elisha prayed to the Lord, "Strike this army with blindness." So he struck them with blindness, as Elisha had asked. (2 Kings 6:15–18)

The angels carried out these assignments. They were also the ones who were on the chariots surrounding Elisha's enemies. This is how powerful the verse we are talking about when Jesus acknowledges us before angels. You have the right to be heard and ask God for intervention to your particular situation. This story happened before Jesus was here on the earth. Elisha was a prophet of God and able to call these things into existence. He was chosen by God to show the world how things could be done here on earth. We are now the chosen people of God who are able to tap into this very same power once we have been chosen by God. When you receive the knowledge of God and how to tap into the power of God, you too will be able to tap into the spiritual realm and ask angels to help you in your time of need.

Are not all angels ministering spirits sent to serve those who will inherit salvation? (Heb. 1:14)

We have angels ministering to us since we will inherit salvation. They are all around us, showing the glory and power of God on a daily basis. They minister in different ways to me on a daily basis. Sometimes they just want me to know they are there and want me to smile, knowing they have given me a spiritual wink, "Hey, we are here." Other times they lead me down a path of wisdom and knowledge by giving me a revelation about God's Word. And other times they want me to realize that I am special, and they show me this by giving me favor wherever I go.

Let me start off with the first statement: the angels giving me a spiritual wink. They do this quite often. I will be driving to work and listening to my Christian music, and they will play one of my songs that God knows is a song that lets me know God is thinking about me. They know exactly what those songs are because I play them almost every day. They will also show me numbers that make me laugh because, again, I know they are speaking to me. I will get a receipt total of like $4.44. Or sometimes I look at my phone to see what time it is, and it will be 1:11 or 3:33 or even 5:55, and I know that they are communicating with me to pay attention. We have fun all the time talking with each other. I know and understand they are there, and they want to let me know that they are there talking back to me.

I am trying to grow spiritually by studying God's word and wanting to learn more and to get closer to God. I will study a specific topic and want to get a greater understanding of it, and the angels lead me to certain scriptures when studying the Bible. I also like to see things on YouTube from other Christian speakers or videos of other people. While watching or studying a topic, I will almost always end up finding what I am searching for when doing my studying. I just follow watching the one video that leads to another video, which leads me to another video, which gets me to the video that I need to see with my own eyes. I am still amazed on how God leads me to my answer. I am sure my angels are given the assignment of giving me revelation knowledge. They are here to show me and minister to me what I am searching for in my life. I always have these experiences when I am truly seeking God and His wisdom for my life. I know my angels minister to me by these means so I may understand a little more about God and my destiny.

The last way I know that my angels are watching over me is the favor in my life, which isn't normal in my case. Let's call it supernatural. When at work, I mostly leave the premises for lunch. I used to go to lunch with our cosmetics manager before she was promoted. We would go out to eat, and I drove most of the time to the restaurant. Well, I started to notice this strange thing happening over and over. I started to notice that I would continually park in the front space right by the entrance of the restaurant. I called the prophet and told him of this favor I was getting at every place I would go. He proceeded to tell me that this happens to him all the time. I said, "This is new for me." He told me how this process works in the spiritual realm. He said, "The angels get you to leave your store at a particular time. When you leave, another angel is telling the person in that spot, 'I am going to park. It's your time to finish up to leave.'" Then when I get to my location, the spot is ready for me. I know that sound like a lot of work for angels to do for me to park, but that's what happens.

I would go to the restaurant and really start to pay attention to what's happening. The cosmetic manager started to notice as well. We both were so surprised to see this happen over and over. I told her what the prophet told me, and she was amazed. One day we went to eat, and the restaurant was packed to the max, so I was just trying to find a place not necessarily by the door due to how many cars where in the parking lot. She asked, "What are you doing?" I said, "Here is a parking spot." She said, "So you better go to the front of the door because I know there is a spot for us there." Sure enough, there was a spot in this packed restaurant right by the entrance.

I now go to lunch with the market manager. We went to a restaurant that has about twenty parking spots at their facility. As we pulled around the corner, I couldn't see one parking spot available. I said, "We might have to go to another restaurant due to no parking spots available." Well, here in Texas, lots of people drive trucks. I decided to drive into the parking facility to just check it out. To my coworker and my surprise, on the other side of this big truck was a parking just for us. Oh, by the way, it was right by the entrance of the restaurant! These two people wouldn't let me try to park far away because they had seen how angels provide favor for me even in the simple things in life.

CHAPTER 11

Understanding the Truth

What if all our lives, we weren't taught the truth, not because we aren't allowed to know the truth but because it has been distorted for thousands of years? Actually, the powers in control didn't want us to know the truth because they wouldn't be able to control us.

Let's go back into history for a moment. In the year AD 325, Constantine, the ruler at that time, got together with the religious leaders to figure a way on how to control the people back then. You can study this in your history books. I would recommend you to do your own research because it is the foundation of how we are controlled today. They got together and formed a secret society to hide and destroy all books and literature that were relevant at that time in history. As we know, back in those times, not many people could read, so they were dependent on those who could read. It's not like today where almost everybody can read. This is where the illuminati were first formed in the world. They became in power with the religious leaders and the king Constantine to control the people of the world. They did this by controlling the books and teaching of the people. They all formed this secret society to do this that is still in existence in the world today. They had done a wonderful job of controlling the people and how the stories are taught in the world today. They are the ones who wrote history and how it looks in today's society. They had mastered how to control man in every area of the world. They are still at it today. We have lost many books that were once in the Bible. They have eliminated about forty-four books that we can confirm from past time. They are still in control of history and what we know about it in this present day and age.

Did you ever wonder why the book of Enoch is not in the Bible, the person who God loved so much that he took Enoch to heaven without experiencing death? And we only have a couple of verses about his life. That just doesn't make sense. He should have a very well-detailed book that shows us how to live correctly in this world. Yet his book somehow didn't make it into the Bible. So what are they trying to hide from us, common people, who really want to know and understand about God? Why is this book of such importance missing? What vital information are they trying to hide from us? We must know that there is something of great value that this society is trying to hide from us. We must wake up and understand that this world operates on different principles than we think. We must understand, that is what they are trying to conceal from us.

Let's look at another book that was eliminated from the Bible, and that would be the book of Thomas. This book is so different than the other books that the disciples wrote. This book actually teaches us some very powerful insight on how Jesus taught the disciples. Thomas spoke the meanings of how things operate in the spiritual realm. He told us powerful truths that we just rediscovered when they found the Dead Sea scrolls. In these writings, they found the book of Thomas. They found other documents that give a better describing of what things were taught back in those days. They teach truth and power that comes from God's Word in our lives. They let us know and see how things really work in our world that we live in today. We are better able to understand how things work and the ability to tap into the spiritual realm. One of the saying in the book of Thomas reads, "Let not him who seeks desist until he finds. When he finds, he will be troubled; when he is troubled, he will marvel, and he will reign over the universe." When we find what we have been seeking, it will trouble us because it goes against what I/ we have been taught. And when the truth will be realized, it will marvel me/us. And then I/we will know *our power that I have supreme reign over my life and everything in it!*

I/we can truly experience heaven here on earth.

This is a powerful statement that I have personally experienced. When I first met the prophet, I was in awe and amazement. I thought some of his sayings were a little out there—well, let's say, unbelievable! I took the good stuff and disregarded all the other stuff. After talking to him for a month or so, I got very angry and discouraged with God. I, at one point, said, "This is all unbelievable, and I don't want anything to do with God or the prophet at all." I didn't call or talk to him for about a week or so. I didn't listen to Christian music or even read my Bible. I refused to do any of the things I normally do—pray, read the Bible, or even listen to Christian music—due to all these lies I had been taught throughout my life. After calming down during that week or so, I called the prophet in a calmer state of mind. I told him what I was going through, and he understood that all this was new, and I needed time to think, be angry with God, and think some more. I truly was going to give up on God at one point during this time. I came to realize that once I was unplugged from the world system, I was going through the shock of this revelation.

I was troubled, just like the verse from the book of Thomas states. I was very troubled! The prophet went on to tell me that I was warned about this before I decided to enter into this wisdom and knowledge that had been hidden from me. When this first occurred, I didn't know anything about the book of Thomas. I was like a plane, ready to crash and burn. I then started to take the prophet's teaching and really study what he was trying to teach me. And just like the verse state, I was amazed and marveled at the teaching and things he was showing me. I started to realize the power that dwelled within me and how to tap into this power.

To really understand these teachings, you will need to study those two books and see how the teachings are totally different from the present Bible, not that the Bible isn't true. This just goes on to give us a more in-depth teaching that this secret society and religion doesn't want you to know about because then you will become a threat to them.

What we need to know is that there is more to God that is in us than we realize. We are a powerful descendant of God, and we have the ability to tap into this power once we understand it in our lives. The truth about man and the power within us has been hidden for centuries. We are here to unveil these mysteries so you can harness this power from the spiritual realm. You will be amazed at what you are able to accomplish here on earth. We can decide our destiny! We can control our future because of God within us. We have the same power and authority that Jesus had, yet we walk in ignorance because no one has taught us about this truth. How would your life change if you understood all these truths and were able to harness them in your life? You would be able to walk with more confidence, knowing that you effected the outcome in your life. You have that power inside of you. There are many mistakes we have made in life because we don't understand life to its fullest. My angels have helped me and guided me to all these truths. They have revealed to the prophet these mysteries, and he has shared them with me.

This truth that you don't understand is a wonderful experience in your life. You will start to understand why you are here and your purpose. You might not like the process when you are going through it, but once the initial shock is overcome, life becomes much better. I have now come to this state in my life. I now continually seek wisdom, knowledge, and understanding. It's a drive that consumes my life. I try to relax some days, but my spirit wants more and more.

CHAPTER 12

Impactful Scriptures

> You, dear children, are from God and have
> overcome them, because the one who is in you
> is greater than the one who is in the world.
>
> Ye are of God, little children, and have
> overcome them: because greater is he that is
> in you, than he that is in the world.
>
> —1 John 4:4 KJV

Here we have this verse in two different translations.

Both verses are letting us know that greater is He that is in us than he that is in the world. This is very interesting since most people are not acting like this in life. We read about this scripture and say, "Amen!" But when you look at their lives, they are living in pain, distress, lack, and many more issues. Why? Is this scripture just for certain people or the special people? This scripture is a top-ten-sermon scripture to inspire the people of God but without power to back it up. These are the same people who go to battle and come back in defeat. So is this a false scripture or just a suggestion? Is there any truth to this scripture? And if so, why are so many people struggling? What power inside of us are they talking about? Let us take a closer look into this scripture.

I asked the prophet of God about this scripture, and we have had many good discussions about this topic on several different levels. We will keep it simple in this book so as to give you the entry-level teaching about this subject. Christ lives inside of us, so He is part of the Trinity. So that means, God lives inside of us as well. So we have the power of God living inside of our bodies. God created everything and has all power. Well, once we understand this, then we can understand that we have that same power within us. All of God's energy dwells in us! Well, not all his energy, but what He gives us is enough to do and defeat the enemy: the ability to create and speak things into existence, the ability to cooperate with angels on our behalf, the ability to heal people, and so much more. We just don't believe this statement or scripture, so we can't access the power we are entitled to and use it in our lives. We don't think we have power or try to use it, not totally believing it works. We are double-minded. And God says, when this happens, don't expect anything. When we do understand the meaning and power that dwell within us, you become a force that the devil wants no part of you. You have accessed the spiritual realm and now are a weapon of God here on earth. You will walk like one of the mighty men of God: Elijah, Elisha, Moses, Solomon, Peter, or Paul, just to name a few. They didn't walk in fear and intimidation; they walked as powerful men of God, knowing the power that was within them. When we understand the word *greater*, we can understand the verse.

Greater

1. unusually or comparatively large in size or dimensions:

A *great* fire destroyed nearly half the city.

2. large in number; numerous:

Great hordes of tourists descend on Europe each summer.

3. unusual or considerable in degree, power, intensity, etc.:

great pain

4. *Comparative larger in size or dimensions; unusual or considerable in degree, power or intensity.*

That is in me, then he that is in the world.

Look at the verse now. Jesus is letting us know, the enemy doesn't have a chance when we realize what is inside of us! So you are very powerful. The Creator of heaven and earth, all that is seen and unseen, is inside of you. We are a powerful weapon for the kingdom of God. You are not here by accident. You are not here for no reason. You were created to fulfill a purpose and to learn God's ways. We must understand how God operates in His kingdom to understand our world here on earth. We must understand the ways the universe operates to access its potential. And this all resides inside of us. We must know ourselves because a key to accessing this mystery lies within us. More on this at a later time.

> "Very truly I tell you, whoever believes in me will do the works I have been doing, and they will do even greater things than these, because I am going to the Father. And I will do whatever you ask in my name, so that the Father may be glorified in the Son. You may ask me for anything in my name, and I will do it." (John 14:12–14)

What is Jesus trying to show us in this scripture? Another wonderful scripture that all Christians know, yet it doesn't work in our lives. We get excited hearing this scripture and say "Amen, hallelujah, glory to God!" yet have *no power* in our life!

We fail to understand what the scripture is trying to convey to us. Jesus is letting us know that everything He did, we can do greater to those who believe in him. We must believe in Him and that He has given us the ability to do all the things He did and greater!

Yet I don't see ministers healing people or feeding thousands of people with a few fish and some bread. I don't see people turning water into wine. I don't see people raising others from the grave. Why isn't any of this going on if Jesus said it could be done and greater? This wasn't one of the disciplines who said this statement. This was Jesus Christ, the son of God. Your thoughts and words have spiritual power that you wouldn't believe, unless you know how to use it. I have tested this fact or theory, and it works. Why would God give us a glimpse into our possibilities if we aren't able to understand or use His words and teachings. What is He talking about within us? What is within us? It's the ability to access the spiritual realm and activate it for our purpose. We have so much power within us that we could do these mighty things Jesus tells us about. We must understand that there is power and authority inside of us that the spiritual realm understands and acts upon. We must first have the thought of what we want to happen and then see it happening already, and it will manifest. I know it sounds crazy, but it's not. We, you and me, can have whatever desire when we think and meditate on it. Our mind is so powerful when you think about it. We can imagine things into existence! We have that power inside of us to accomplish this with the help of the spiritual realm. Angels are there, waiting for us to put them to work, wanting us to pray for something so they can be put into action. When we pray, we are speaking into the spiritual realm for there to be a reaction to the words we are sending into the spiritual realm. Our words are very powerful. The Bible says in Proverbs 18:21, "The tongue has the power of life and death, and those who love it will eat its fruit."

What do you think the Bible is trying to tell us here? Life is the power of our tongue. We create life with our partner to produce children. Well, we create life in the natural with our words. We cause life to be created by words! And these words come from our thoughts. So we must protect our thoughts so our words will be productive. Once we speak our thoughts, and they become words, we will eat the fruit of it. There is a saying, which goes like this: If you think you can, then you can. If you think you can't, then you can't. Either way you are correct.

So I want to give God the glory when I call things into existence. I have the qualities of God, so I am able to do the same things God can do because I have the same DNA as my

Father. I have an imagination like my Father, so I can think of wonderful things and things that would help others. And I have a tongue to speak it into existence, so my God can get the glory! Why aren't we doing things in our lifetime to give God the glory and show how we are the children of God at the same time? Why is this scripture not a living scripture to us in the world? We aren't waiting for God; He is waiting on us to start doing things for His kingdom. We need to speak and believe that His words are true and living in our lives. We must believe that when we ask for things in Jesus's name, He is there, going to the Father with our petitions. Jesus is standing in the gap for us. He wants us to have things here on earth, such as a whole family, health, money, a house, and much more, if we put God first. He is wanting us to succeed so He can get the glory. He doesn't mind us having things as long as the things don't have us.

> The thief comes only to steal and
> kill and destroy; I have come that they
> may have life, and have it to the full
> (abundant life). (John 10:10)

Does this sound like we should be struggling in life down here on earth? No, it doesn't. It sounds like we should be living life to the full or abundance. There should be no reason why we should be struggling in life if we declare this scripture over our lives. We must remind God what He promised us while we live here on earth. We use our words to live like God intended us to live, nothing less! Our responsibility is to understand what this scripture is trying to tell us. Jesus came for us to understand Him and what He did for us. He came down to reconnect us to God and the spiritual realm. He came to teach us in depth how things work, and

He demonstrates how they work in the spiritual realm. We must look at His life and understand the hidden meanings that are in plain sight. We must not only read the scriptures but also look for the hidden meanings in His teachings. Then we must ask ourselves, Why did He say this? What is He trying to tell us? What is He showing us in His demonstration of His powers? What lessons are we supposed to learn from this teaching?

What does it mean to live life to its fullest or have abundant life? Is it to live stress-free? Is it to have lots of resources? Is it to be successful? Is it to be full of wisdom, knowledge, and understanding? Is it to be full of love? Or could it be all the above? It all depends on how you look at things in life. Some people see the glass half full, while other see it half empty. What is your perspective? The better question is, how does God see it? How we see things is our perspective to the situation, but God sees things from a whole different perspective. We see the trees in the forest, and God sees the forest from the view of heaven. It's totally different than ours. God wants us to learn about Him! He wrote a whole book for us to study and understand Him. We are to look and seek the meaning of His teachings!

CHAPTER 13

A Touch from the Prophet

We have already talked about the power of God. Now we are going to give some amazing examples of His power!

Earlier in the book, I told the story of scales being removed from my eyes. I am still amazed at how this happened and now all the possibilities that happen in my life because of this removal of the scales. Here are some examples from the Bible that go along with this story so you may know that it is possible. In the book of Second Kings, it states the following:

When the servant of the man of God got up and went out early the next morning, an army with horses and chariots had surrounded the city. "Oh no, my lord! What shall we do?" the servant asked.

"Don't be afraid," the prophet answered. "Those who are with us are more than those who are with them."

And Elisha prayed, "Open his eyes, Lord, so that he may see." Then the Lord opened the servant's eyes, and he looked and saw the hills full of horses and chariots of fire all around Elisha. (2 Kings 6:15–17)

As he neared Damascus on his journey, suddenly a light from heaven flashed around him. He fell to the ground and heard a voice say to him, "Saul, Saul, why do you persecute me?"

"Who are you, Lord?" Saul asked.

"I am Jesus, whom you are persecuting," he replied. "Now get up and go into the city, and you will be told what you must do."

The men traveling with Saul stood there speechless; they heard the sound but did not see anyone. Saul got up from the ground, but when he opened his eyes he could see nothing. (Acts 9:3–8)

Then Ananias went to the house and entered it. Placing his hands on Saul, he said, "Brother Saul, the Lord—Jesus, who appeared to you on the road as you were coming here—has sent me so that you may see again and be filled with the Holy Spirit." Immediately, something like scales fell from Saul's eyes, and he could see again. (Acts 9:17–18)

These are the two examples of what happened to me that day when the prophet spoke to me that the scales would fall so I could see. I wanted to show you this so you could see that scales on our eyes exist, and they can also be removed from our eyes. What I want you to understand is that there is natural blindness where you can't see anything, and there is spiritual blindness where you can't see what God has hidden. There is a spiritual realm that exists at the same time we are existing. It is happening right now. Where you are, the spiritual realm is there. Angels, good and evil, are right there, living among us. We are coexisting together, yet we can't see them unless the spiritual eyes are opened to see them. We must be fully aware of these things so we can better understand God's kingdom. My eyes are able to see things that most people in this world are unaware of because of this removal of scales from my eyes. When I read and study, certain scriptures jump off the pages to show me a hidden truth about God's Word. It also lets me know that I need to dig deep into this scripture and focus on what God is revealing to me. It also opens up the scripture to the secrets that are hidden in the Bible that normal people can't see. I am so amazed how it works. I have read certain scriptures hundreds of times, and I thought I understood them until I truly read them and see things like I never saw before!

At first it was mind-blowing. Then the more I read, the more I understood. It is such a gift I received and drives me to learn more about God like never before. The only problem is, the prophet tells me I am kindergartner level in my education. I look at it as good because that means there are much more to learn about God. I also look at it like, I truly didn't understand anything about God and thought I was an educated man who loved God and studied His word. I had been teaching and giving sermons for His glory yet didn't see things like I see them now. So I must have been teaching baby-food sermons. I thought they were excellent before and not so much now. Now, when I teach, people are fascinated with my teaching because I now see things differently. I teach differently about what the Bible is saying. I understand different things that I didn't understand before. People are seeking the truth! Our spirit knows the difference when they hear the truth. It sometimes goes against our tradition of religion. But didn't Jesus go against religion in His time? Well, it's the same now. Not everyone will agree with what I am trying to convey to the people, and that's their right. I just want to tell you, my experiences with God after having my encounter with the prophet.

How would you like to have access to spiritual knowledge at your disposal anytime you like? I have that ability when I talk to the prophet. He teaches me about God and the things of heaven and earth. He is able to speak with angels on a daily basis and does several times a day and ask questions about anything he likes. Those are his friends. We have friends or family who we visit and talk to. Well, that's who he talks to and are his friends.

Let me give you an example of this so you won't think I am making this up. So one day, the prophet and I were having a conversation, and my son came over, so I let him talk to the prophet. The prophet told my son, "I like your angel" because he makes sure my son prospers on his endeavors. He makes money and doesn't even have to try. I was skeptical about this particular word given about my son. I am not sure how long later, but my wife, my son, his son, and I went to an Astros baseball game. During the game, the Astros organization sold raffle tickets for charity to raise money for the community. All the money raised for that game was split fifty-fifty. The fans had a chance to win 50 percent of the total money raised. It so happened that the money for that night was around $24,000, which meant the winner would get around $12,000, not bad for a $20 investment. My wife and I purchased tickets so I could put into practice what I had been learning about thinking to win and seeing myself win. Well, I didn't remember my son was with me and what the prophet said about my son's angel. It was his first time to purchase a ticket, and I'd be darn if he didn't win the money. I was in shock! He actually won the money. I remembered what the prophet said about his angel. He doesn't even have to try to make money, and he does. Wow, that was a shocker to see it happen as the prophet had said. Now you can't tell me that was luck or by chance. If you believe that, I have a bridge to sell you in the dessert. Haha.

Today was a strange day in that I am becoming more in tune with the spiritual realm. Two days ago, one of the store vendors asked me to purchase a raffle ticket to win either a steer, heifer, pig, goat, or rabbit for $100. It was for the FFA so they could raise money for the school and their program. I told her sure, that I would go in half with another manager. Well, today I went with the other manager to play golf, and on my way home, I was thinking about winning either the steer or heifer. I didn't say anything out loud on my way home about this; I was just thinking about it. So I got home, and I was talking to my wife about the day and planning what we wanted to accomplish for the day when my phone rang. The phone number was a number I didn't recognize, and it wasn't a number from my contacts. The number was from a town about thirty miles away. I thought it might be about a house, since my wife and I were looking at homes, so this could be one of those numbers. I answered the phone and came to find out it was a guy who had attended one of our church's men's camps. He moved to the Dallas area because he want to raise cattle and get into that business. I hadn't talked to him in about a year. He said I came into his mind, and he wanted to tell me how and why I came into his mind. He knew I had a food truck business. Food truck business had called him since there was a lack of meat processing due the virus that was going on, and he started the business and could get me meat at a reasonable price. I said, "We'll send you the information, and I will take a look at it." What are the odds of that happening, somebody calling me about meat to purchase when I was just thinking about that today on my way home? You can't tell me God doesn't know my thoughts and then sends the answer to those thoughts. Wow!

> You have searched me, Lord, and
you know me.
> You know when I sit and when I
rise; you perceive my thoughts from afar.
> You discern my going out and my
lying down; you are familiar with all my
ways.
> Before a word is on my tongue you,
Lord, know it completely. (Ps. 139:1–4)

God knows what we think before we even speak it. Well, that happened to me today. I know there is a God, and He is with me every step of my way.

> I love those who love me, and those
who seek me find me. (Prov. 8:17)

> You will seek me and find me when
you seek me with all your heart. (Jer. 29:13)

How many of you are willing to truly seek God? If you seek Him, you will find Him. Seek Him with all of your heart. The scripture states that God is willing to be found after we seek Him. He wants to show us great and mighty things, but we have to seek. We must be willing to surrender our lives to know the truth. We could have been a good person or a bad person, like Paul who killed Christians. God wants a personal relationship with us. Are you willing to seek Him and learn the truth?

> To the Jews who had believed him, Jesus said, "If you hold to my teaching, you are really my disciples. Then you will know the truth, and the truth will set you free." (John 8:31–32)

A lot of us don't want to know the truth! We are happy being the religious leaders of our times, which oppose Jesus. When we hear the truth, we don't want to believe it, even when there is evidence with miracles and signs. Jesus did all the above and was rejected by society. Then they killed Him in the name of religion. Most people reading this book will be skeptical about the teachings I am presenting, even with all this evidence in front of you, and that is fine. And I will explain why in one second. But there are a few of you who really want to understand and know the truth. Then you will have to make up your mind that God's words and teachings have power. That same power resides inside of you. And to the others who still can't grasp the truth, here is why.

> For many are invited, but few are chosen. (Matt. 22:14)

You might like this story of the wedding banquet. You have been called but not chosen. You have called to come and know about God but only on a milk level or surface level, nothing deep. Then others will be called to go a little deeper and know scriptures, be able to quote different verse, and will know the Bible, but it is only head knowledge. Some will become preachers, teachers, priest, ministers, and even theologians. They will tell you all that they know and understand, and some will have a very good in-depth conversation. Yet God speaks to the heart! They may even claim that He is in their heart, and I believe He is, yet the heart connects you to the spiritual realm. Your heart plays a vital role in our relationship with God.

CHAPTER 14

Our Heart

We must understand that our heart and emotions play a huge role when we pray to God. He is moved by both of these factors. Here are some scriptures about the heart.

For wisdom will enter your heart,
and knowledge will be pleasant to your
soul. (Prov. 2:10)

This is an interesting statement that many people overlook when they read this verse. It states, wisdom will enter your heart. Isn't it interesting that wisdom doesn't enter our brain, where our knowledge is stored for learning? When I learn something, either by experience or other books, my mind is learning and growing. The brain is retaining knowledge and wisdom for us to grow. Yet the scripture states that wisdom will enter our hearts. What is the purpose of this statement? Did God mean to say *brain*? Do we understand that the things about life and how we learn is because we have a brain? I don't remember studying anatomy where the heart learns something. I remember where it is, the muscle that pumps life into us on a continuous basis. Blood comes in one way and leave out the other side, taking oxygen in and pumping it throughout the body. Never did I study that it was where wisdom is stored. How can that be?

Where is that found in the medical books? How is your heart able to obtain information or so-called wisdom? What does your heart do with this wisdom? Why doesn't your brain obtain this wisdom that God is talking about? Does our heart have a memory? These are some serious questions for us to think about. I know the heart can feel pain and hurt when we lose a loved one, but how is that connected with wisdom? By chance, is our heart a second brain. Maybe the heart is connected to the spiritual realm that we forgot about. God wouldn't tell us this in scripture if He didn't mean what He said. He is telling us something of great importance, and it is our job to seek it out and find the hidden truth about this scripture.

> My son, do not forget my teaching,
> but keep my commands in your heart,
> for they will prolong your life many years
> and bring you peace and prosperity.
> Let love and faithfulness never leave
> you; bind them around your neck, write
> them on the tablet of your heart.
> Then you will win favor and a good
> name in the sight of God and man.
> Trust in the Lord with all your heart
> and lean not on your own understand-
> ing; in all your ways submit to him, and
> he will make your paths straight. (Prov.
> 3:1–6)

These verses tell us a lot about the heart. Keep my commands in your heart. How can we do this? Aren't we supposed to know the commands and have them in our brain? God says, have the commands in our hearts. Our brain is like a computer that we can access information and store things, like memories, good or bad; experiences that we learn from; education that helps us in life that we should remember and helps us when the situation comes up again. So our brain is like a place where we have storage and memory that we can obtain to help us through life. Our heart is a muscle that pumps blood and oxygen that keeps us alive. I wonder how we are supposed to store something in a muscle. Could it be that it is more than a muscle? Maybe it's a place more complex than a muscle to store something. It must have space available to store something—let's say, the capacity to store something. Then does it have a memory to recall things as well? Why would I store something in the heart and not be able to recall it when needed? So is our heart acting like a second brain? I ask again. When we store the commands in our heart, it comes with some promises: long life, peace, and prosperity! Wow, what an amazing God we serve! By keeping His commands in our hearts, we are guaranteed long life, peace, and prosperity! Now that's amazing to me. I don't know about you, but I am excited right now to know this truth about God! But wait, there is more in these scriptures.

> Let love and faithfulness never leave
> you; bind them around your neck, write
> them on the tablet of your heart. Let *love
> and faithfulness* never leave you!

Love
Definition of *love*

1.
    a)
        1)   strong affection for another arising out of kinship or personal ties

maternal *love* for a child

        2)   attraction based on sexual desire: affection and tenderness felt by lovers

After all these years, they are still very much in *love*.

        3)   affection based on admiration, benevolence, or common interests

love for his old schoolmates

    b)   an assurance of affection

Give her my *love*.

2.   warm attachment, enthusiasm, or devotion

love of the sea

3.
    a)   the object of attachment, devotion, or admiration

Baseball was his first *love*.

    b)
        1) a beloved person: DARLING —often used as a term of endearment
        2) *British* —used as an informal term of address

4. unselfish loyal and benevolent (see BENEVOLENT sense 1a) concern for the good of another: such as
    a) the fatherly concern of God for humankind
    b) brotherly concern for others

Faithfulness
Definition of *faithful*

1. steadfast in affection or allegiance: LOYAL

a *faithful* friend

2. firm in adherence to promises or in observance of duty: CONSCIENTIOUS

a *faithful* employee

3. given with strong assurance: BINDING

a *faithful* promise

4. true to the facts, to a standard, or to an original

a *faithful* copy

5. *obsolete*: full of faith

We are to bind these two truths around our neck and write them on the tablets of our heart. We are to show love and faithfulness to our God and to man as well, always carrying them with us and also writing them on our heart so we can engrave these truths on our heart, and our heart is all right with this. It's kind of like a chalkboard on our heart, saying love and faithfulness! So far, we can store stuff in our heart and also write things on our heart.

Then you will win favor and a good name in the sight of God and man.

So now we have two more things that happen when we do this:

- We win favor
- A good name

With two beings:

- God
- Man

By keeping His commands in our heart, we are guaranteed

1. Long life
2. Peace
3. Prosperity
4. Favor
5. Good name

Trust in the Lord with all your heart and lean not on your own understanding.

Trust
Definition of *trust*

1.
    a)   assured reliance on the character, ability, strength, or truth of someone or something
    b)   one in which confidence is placed
2.
    a)   dependence on something future or contingent: HOPE
    b)   reliance on future payment for property (such as merchandise) delivered: CREDIT

bought furniture on *trust*

3.
    a)   a property interest held by one person for the benefit of another
    b)   a combination of firms or corporations formed by a legal agreement

especially: one that reduces or threatens to reduce competition

4.
    a)   CARE, CUSTODY

the child committed to her *trust*

    b)
        1)   a charge or duty imposed in faith or confidence or as a condition of some relationship

2)   something committed or entrusted to
one to be used or cared for in the inter-
est of another

So we must *trust* in the Lord with all our heart, having
that assurance in God that He is looking after our best inter-
est. We must do that with all our heart. The means, completely with all emotions, mental, and physical parts of us
100 percent in!

Lean not on our own understanding! That is a hard
thing to do since we think we know and understand all things.
When in reality, we don't understand hardly anything. We
think we are so intelligent, yet we can't even get out of messes
we create ourselves. We ask others for advice, thinking they
are so smart. In reality, they aren't any smarter than us! We
are leaning on their understanding instead of God's wisdom
and understanding! Remember the scripture that states:

"For my thoughts are not your
thoughts, neither are your ways my
ways," declares the Lord.
"As the heavens are higher than
the earth, so are my ways higher than
your ways and my thoughts than your
thoughts." (Isa. 55:8–9)

Remember how I talked about God's ways. What if the
way God does things is totally different than what we perceive things here on earth? Why would God make sure to
put that scripture in the Bible if we weren't supposed to read
it and understand this verse? So when we trust in God in
His way and lean not on our understanding, there must be
a point to this statement. Maybe our thinking and thoughts

are so much lower than God that He wants us to trust in Him! He is giving us a key to the ways we should go. Listen to where He is trying to guide us, and discover what He is trying to teach us, and we will do well in our life.

> My son, pay attention to what I say;
> turn your ear to my words.
> Do not let them out of your sight,
> keep them within your heart;
> for they are life to those who find
> them and health to one's whole body.
> Above all else, guard your heart, for
> everything you do flows from it. (Prov. 4:20–23)

So what is the scripture trying to explain to us in this verse? It is letting us know that we need to pay attention to His Word! We need to listen to what God is saying to us. We get so busy that we miss His word most of the time. We are so busy with life that it seems that God is an afterthought, when God should be our first and foremost thought! We should keep His words in our sight—that means, always looking at His word and what He is trying to say to us. We have the TV, work, kids, and sports as our focus and lose what God is attempting to teach us. We need to keep His word as our main focus. Once they are our main focus, we must keep them in our hearts. Here we go again with the heart being a storage unit. We must store the living words, God's word, in our hearts. Just as the heart supplies our body with life, the word of God supplies our spirit with life, the life that we really need to understand, God, and the ways of God, not the human ways but the ways of the Creator of the universe, the one who created all things seen and unseen, the power of the

Almighty, for they are life to those who find them and health to one's whole body.

When we study the human anatomy, the heart is the main function or center of life for the body. When the heart fails, everything else fails, and we no longer have life but will pass on or will no longer exist here on earth.

God's word is life to our spiritual man and connects us to the Creator. But we must find God's Word. When we find God's Word, then we will have His promises, which is life and health in one's body. So why are we focusing on other priorities in life before we find God's Word? Are we just existing, not living at all? Yet I am breathing and doing things, such as working, playing, enjoying life. But God says I am not living. His word must do more than we think. It must activate something in our spiritual man that we don't realize. Because once we do this, God says we are living. Let that soak in for a while!

Above all else, guard your heart, for everything you do flows from it.

Definition of *guard* (verb)
transitive verb

1. to protect an edge of with an ornamental border
2.
    a) to protect from danger especially by watchful attention: make secure

police *guarding* our cities

    b) to stand at the entrance of as if on guard or as a barrier
    c) to tend to carefully: PRESERVE, PROTECT

guarded their privacy

3.   *archaic*: ESCORT
4.
  a)   to watch over so as to prevent escape, disclo-
       sure, or indiscretion

guarded the prisoners

  b)   to attempt to prevent (an opponent) from
       playing effectively or scoring

intransitive verb: to watch by way of caution or defense:
stand guard

We protect from danger and are watchful of our hearts. So who are we defending our hearts from? And what do they want with our hearts? Some very interesting questions.

Well, long life comes from our heart. We also store wisdom in our heart. Health comes from our heart. Favor is in our heart with God and man. Prosperity comes from the heart. Peace comes from our heart. So as you can see, our heart is a very important organ that God puts a great value on in our life. Therefore, we must do our part to guard and protect it from the enemy of this world. We are at battle every day for our heart, and some days we win and other days, not so much. We have all had a broken heart, and we understand the pain of that moment in time. We must be strong and alert about the devises of the enemy.

> The crucible for silver and the
> furnace for gold, but the Lord tests the
> heart. (Prov. 17:3)

The heart of the discerning acquires knowledge, for the ears of the wise seek it out. (Prov. 18:15)

The purposes of a person's heart are deep waters, but one who has insight draws them out. (Prov. 20:5)

Pay attention and turn your ear to the sayings of the wise; apply your heart to what I teach, for it is pleasing when you keep them in your heart and have all of them ready on your lips. (Prov. 22:17–18)

CHAPTER 15

Conclusion

The story you have read in this book is an experience I have personally gone through and experienced. I wouldn't have believed it or would have some serious doubts if it wasn't my life. I have come to the conclusion that me seeking God connected me with the prophet of God. He reminds me that it was my prayers that drew Him to me and not me to Him. I would have never met the prophet unless I was doing the will of God and seeking the truth about God. So if you are wanting to experience the truth, you must be seeking God with all your heart, mind, and soul. God does answer prayers when we seek Him first, just as His word states.

> But seek first his kingdom and his
> righteousness, and all these things will be
> given to you as well. (Matt. 6:33)

I did that and now have access to some insights that I was unaware of before. I have gained or have been granted wisdom, knowledge, and understanding of the kingdom of God. I am learning about God's kingdom and how to access the power from this kingdom. I am still trying to understand why I was chosen by God for this adventure that I am now exploring and involved in. I am truly amazed of what I have learned and experienced because of my encounter with the prophet. I have tested and put into action what I have been taught and seen the hand of God move in my life.

I am not here to change or influence your religion or to try to convert you into what I believe. I am here to tell you a story of what has happened in my life. It is up to you to decide what you want to believe or not believe. I am just letting you know that there is a God, and He is real. I have always known this; I just now have experienced more than I have ever thought before and believed to experience more as I continue to grow in this wisdom, knowledge, and understanding. I am learning that we have all been taught only what was passed on for centuries from religion. We must also look at everything that is before us when trying to understand God. We must question things we don't understand, like how the pyramids got here and what their purpose is. I know the Word of God is the most important thing because it is the center of our beliefs, yet there are many other books that we must also look at that coincide with what God is trying to show us. We can't be naive to science, astronomy, mathematics, frequencies, and even aliens when we want to understand God. God created everything! So don't you think we should study everything to understand God and all the information He is sharing with us through these other means? I know I didn't get to share about these topics, but they are there for a reason. We can't be so naive to think that they are there for a distraction. God is everywhere and in everything. So He is in space, as well as in a flower or rainbow. He is in you and me, as well as a building. I could go on forever, but God is everywhere and in all things. Let us try to see God in everything.

I have now the ability to see things in a different perspective since the scales have been removed from my eyes. I am able to understand things that I never saw before when reading the Bible. I now study the Bible and look up things on the Internet. I want to learn as much as possible when it comes to God and my relationship with Him. I feel more connected to Him than I have ever been before. Yet I think there is so much more to understand, and I am not sure I will live long enough to get a full grasp of God. Now, when I seek Him and ask questions, my questions are answered. I go through life, seeing things differently and thinking about all the possibilities that await me. I am accessing the spiritual realm more and more as I grow. I am amazed at how much we are in control of in our lives and how much we don't see or understand. There is a spiritual world out there that most Christians know about on a surface level yet don't try to understand because they think they might access the evil spirits. I need to understand this realm to combat the evil spirits. I need to know the enemy and how to defeat them in their own territory. Jesus took authority over them, and they feared Him. Jesus lives inside of us, so we need to know how to access this authority so we can be effective children of God and take all authority over the enemy. We have the same power as Jesus. Let's figure out how to obtain this power and use it for the glory of God. God needs our help in defeating the enemy here on earth. He uses His children to battle the enemy. He has equipped us with power and authority, so let's learn about this and be effective soldiers for His kingdom.

I hope this book has helped some of you to know about God and the power of God inside of us. I have come a long way since my encounter with the prophet. I hope you can read and understand how important you are and how equipped you are for your God-given destiny. Only you can understand and know the truth that sets you free. Once you understand how the process starts in your life, you will start to understand the deeper things of God. You will see life in a totally different way. You will believe in God in a deeper level and in yourself. God lives inside of us, which is a powerful statement! Many of you will still doubt, and others will gain a new hope and understanding of God. Either way, I am here to encourage you to live life to its fullest, and don't cheat yourself of all you can become while here on earth. I wish you the best on your adventures and hope you fulfill your journey and destiny.

ABOUT THE AUTHOR

Albert V. Salinas Jr. has traveled the world since he grew up an army brat. He had to learn to make friends every one to three years depending on how long his father was stationed at a particular post, which helped him to adapt to any situation. He has known God all his life and doesn't remember a day without God. He served in the army himself and learned many lessons that he uses in life to this day. He is a family man and has seven children and eighteen grandchildren. He is married to Kathy Salinas, who has helped him grow as a man of God. He loves to read, learn, and now write. He loves business and has had several businesses and is currently working on a new venture. He loves helping others with the wisdom he has gained throughout his life and is also called to teach others about God and His love for us all. He is a loving person who is willing to reach out to others. He has gone on several mission trips and preached to many churches while on these trips. He loves seeing God use him to show that God is still alive and well today. He has an aura about him that attracts others to him, which he then helps with life. The gift and talents he has make listening to him teach a pleasure to listen to and easy to understand.